DESIGNING YOUR OWN LIFE

TONY JEARY

Clovercroft Publishing

Designing Your Own Life

©2015 by Tony Jeary

All rights reserved. No part of this book may be reproduced or transmitted in any form or by any means, electronic or mechanical, including photocopying, recording or by any information storage and retrieval system, without permission in writing from the copyright owner.

Published by Clovercroft Publishing, Franklin, Tennessee.

Published in association with Larry Carpenter of Christian Book Services, LLC.
www.christianbookservices.com

Edited by Tawnya Austin and Sara Waller

Cover Design by Eddie Renz

Interior Design by Suzanne Lawing

Printed in the United States of America

978-1-942557-16-6

Introduction

Why This Book (And What It Will Mean to Your Success)

The one thing we can agree on, that we all have in common, is that we all want to live a happy, successful, and fulfilling life. Achieving that can sometimes be elusive, but it doesn't have to be. Ask yourself: is the life you are living right now by accident or on purpose? It should be more on purpose. There are too many people who live a life – at least in some ways – other than the one they want, and it is primarily because they haven't designed the one they want.

Those of you who know me also know my passion for goal setting. Goals are the driving force behind my success, and those I get to encourage are the catalyst for living a happy and fulfilled life I have personally and intentionally designed around the people and things I love and are important to me.

> **Ask yourself: is the life you are living right now by accident or on purpose? It should be more on purpose.**

People get so busy "doing" life that they don't take the time to step back and make sure the life they are "doing" is making them happy and, perhaps even more important, is aligned with their values. Some success may even be happening along the way due to hard work and dedication. Imagine, however, how much your success could be catapulted forward with more intentional activity and real strategic vision.

> **Goals are the driving force behind my success.**

Think for a moment about the most successful organizations you know and respect. What are some things they have in common? According to *Inc. Magazine*, six things super successful companies have in common are 1) setting goals, 2) picking markets,

3) raising capital, 4) building the team, 5) gaining share, and 6) adapting to change. Did you notice what was number one? **Setting goals.** The article goes on to state the importance of short-term, medium-term, and long-term goals.

If this is true with companies, doesn't it make sense that it is true for us as individuals? For example, let's look at how a house is built. Can you imagine contracting someone to build a house for you without having plans? How closely do you think that house would turn out to your desired specifications if there were no blueprints to use in the building process? Even if by some chance the house was worth living in, it is highly doubtful that it would be the house you envisioned for yourself. My good friend, the late Zig Ziglar, once said, "You need a plan to build a house. To build a life, it is even more important to have a plan or goal." I couldn't have said it better.

> YOU NEED A PLAN TO BUILD A HOUSE. TO BUILD A LIFE, IT IS EVEN MORE IMPORTANT TO HAVE A PLAN OR GOAL.

I was very fortunate to have been raised by loving parents who not only encouraged me to go after my own dreams, but to also set goals to achieve them. That fortune continued as I worked with, coached, learned from, and was mentored by many of the top CEOs of the most successful companies in the world over the past 30 years. The sum of that has given me an increased passion for setting goals and expanding the definition of what that even means.

To most people, setting goals means making a list of the things you want to have or accomplish over the next year, five years, or even decade. That's certainly a great start. I would challenge you that there is much more (way more) to actually *Designing Your Own Life*, which is why I wrote this book.

SETTING THE FOUNDATION (TO GET THE MOST FROM THE TOOL)

For the last three decades of working with thousands of top achievers, continued daily study, and tons of research, I've determined that there are nine key things that virtually everyone wants. We use the acronym STRATEGIC to most easily remember them:

Significance – to have meaning

Time – want margin, leverage their time and have flexibility

Relationships – strong, loving people to share life with

Accomplishments – achieving goals

Thrive – happiness impacts the brain positively

Engagement – collaborating and sharing with others

Good Health – stay healthy to live and flourish

Inspired – be motivated and energized to achieve

Capital – have cash flow, reserves and have more financial freedom

All of these nine things work together to create a positive, successful life.

Within these pages, you will find a blueprint for designing your best life. Two major keys are to be intentional about guiding your life in the direction you want it to go, and to be conscious of the people you surround yourself with who can help you achieve your life goals.

When we work with clients, we often share our model of Mastery. It's what we call the Impact Curve. Within this model, there are three levels: Good, Great, and Mastery. Each level will achieve a certain level of success, bringing progressively more and better results.

> TWO MAJOR KEYS ARE TO BE INTENTIONAL ABOUT GUIDING YOUR LIFE IN THE DIRECTION YOU WANT IT TO GO, AND TO BE CONSCIOUS OF THE PEOPLE YOU SURROUND YOURSELF WITH WHO CAN HELP YOU ACHIEVE YOUR LIFE GOALS.

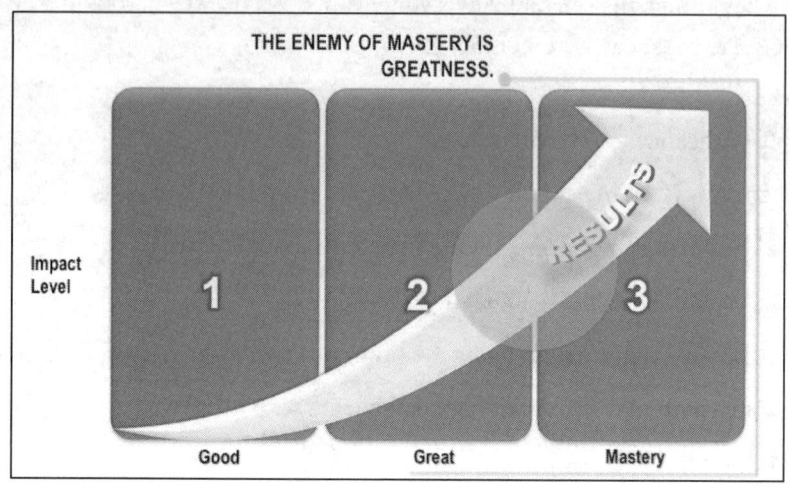

The sections in this book are designed around our model, and have exercises that will take you through each level. As you complete more exercises, you will find your results will multiply.

Why do goals work? (Google "Tony Jeary Why Goals Work" and watch the powerful three-minute video.) Goals work because they help you filter out things that don't matter and stay focused on the things that are important to you. They allow the right things to come into your mind, and hence your life, intentionally. There's a part of your brain called Reticular Activating System (RAS) that actually understands goals. Your RAS is a small group of cells at the base of your brain stem. Its function is to act like a sorting office, evaluating the incoming information (from all senses) and prioritizing what gets into your brain, and eventually what gets your attention. Because your conscious brain can't capture everything, the more serious you are about what you want and focus on, the more your subconscious focuses to achieve it. In fact,

> GOALS WORK BECAUSE THEY HELP YOU FILTER OUT THINGS THAT DON'T MATTER AND STAY FOCUSED ON THE THINGS THAT ARE IMPORTANT TO YOU.

your conscious mind can consume 40 bits of data per second, while your subconscious mind can consume 40 million bits of data per second. That's powerful.

There are three keys to making your goals really work and leveraging your RAS: 1) write down or type with clarity what you really want, 2) visualize it, and 3) employ congruent self-talk for achieving those goals. And, by the way, goals should not just be about what you want to have, but also what you want to experience, share, give, and of course, become.

Actor Jim Carrey did an interview with Oprah Winfrey in 1997, where he shared that in 1992 he had written himself a check for ten million dollars for acting services rendered, and he gave himself three years to accomplish that goal. He dated it Thanksgiving 1995. He put it in his wallet and kept it there; it deteriorated and deteriorated. Then, just before Thanksgiving 1995, he found out he was going to make ten million dollars on *Dumb and Dumber*. It was a pivotal lesson for him in setting personal goals.

Similarly, as I was beginning my career – in fact, when I was 19 years old – I framed and signed a note to myself that stated I would be a millionaire by the age of 25.

I hung it in my bedroom and looked at it daily. I set out to do this when I had barely finished high school. I did know that I was willing to work as hard as it took to reach this goal. It was really my first representation of a Visionboard (what is now called a Resultsboard in my world) or tool, and I actually accomplished this goal in just three short years.

Some who are reading this now

YOU NEED TO MAKE SOME CHANGES IN YOUR THINKING SO YOU ACTUALLY BELIEVE GOAL SETTING WORKS AND WILL WORK FOR YOU.

are ready to jump in and go to another level of goal setting, and that could be you. Or it could be you need to "weed your garden." You need to make some changes in your thinking so you actually believe goal setting works and will work for you.

Goals do work. Goals work because they allow you to get clearer on where you are today and where you want to go, focus on the right things to help achieve your targets, and help you execute for results. In fact, my foundational book, *Strategic Acceleration*, shows clarity, focus, and execution as a powerful methodology for helping both individuals and organizations move toward Mastery and get the right results faster. The same is true for you personally. You have to: 1) get clear, really clear, 2) focus, and 3) take action.

> GOALS DO WORK. GOALS WORK BECAUSE THEY ALLOW YOU TO GET CLEARER ON WHERE YOU ARE TODAY AND WHERE YOU WANT TO GO.

So, a powerful question here is: **"Why don't people set goals?"** One reason is that it just isn't on their radar as being something that is important. Others don't see the benefit of spending the time to set goals or believe that it really leads to more accomplishments. Some people were not introduced to goal setting when they were younger, and it is just not on their *Belief Window*.

A *Belief Window* can be described as a window or filter through which you view the world. On this window are principles (rules, truisms) that were primarily established by your parents in your early life, but then have been influenced by your education, your friends, your church, your experiences, and your career. Sometimes in life, you find that something you had previously believed is no longer valid, so your principle changes. The example I often share from the platform is this: Many grew up with their parents telling them they should always clean their plate. Today, people know that cleaning your plate often leads to overeating. It's actually best to have your plate taken away once you start getting full. Yet, some still feel guilty if they don't clean their plate. It's an old and erroneous principle that many people still believe, and it needs to change on their windows. In the

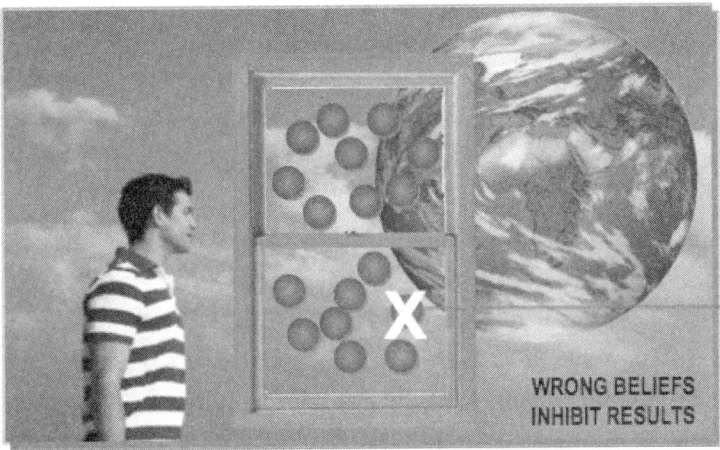

same light, perhaps you need to change what's on your window related to goal setting.

I ask that you keep an open mind when reading these pages so that any pre-conceived ideas you may have about the benefit of setting goals can be expanded. I believe that if you do, you could be headed for your best year ever. And remember, If you design your own life, every day can be like a weekend!

My Story (And Why You Care)

Let's hope my sharing inspires you. There are a handful of specific events or things that significantly shaped my life that will give you an idea of how my passion was born and what set me on the quest I've been on for almost four decades. The first event happened when I was only sixteen years old. My girlfriend's father gave me a book as a gift. That book was *How to Win Friends and Influence People*. It was one of the most influential books of the twentieth century, and it was such an inspiration to me; it opened my mind to the concept of personal development. It is said that Warren Buffet took the Dale Carnegie course by that same name when he was 20 years old, and to this day he has the di-

> IF YOU DESIGN YOUR OWN LIFE, EVERY DAY CAN BE LIKE A WEEKEND!

ploma in his office. It is also listed in my Top 100 Success Books of all time (see **Section 3, Favorite Books of Impact**).

How to Win Friends and Influence People had such an impact, in fact, that it fueled my love for books – both for reading and for authoring books that provide encouragement, inspiration, instruction, and motivation for others to want to be their best.

Another momentous event that helped shape me was meeting Zig Ziglar and the "happy accident" that brought about that meeting. My life coach was talking to me one day and said he thought I should call Zig Ziglar and ask him to have lunch with me. Zig had become very well-known by this point, and to most people the thought that I would actually get connected personally to him was a bit out there – yet I picked up the phone and called his office, and two weeks later I was in his home and we were talking about how he wrote his books. We really got connected. There's more to the story of how that came about.

When I called and got his assistant on the phone and told him I was calling to set up a meeting with Zig, there was a misunderstanding. I was told there was a function at Zig's house in a few days and I was invited. I was given all the proper information; and, although I was somewhat confused, I didn't want to pass up the opportunity to meet and talk with Zig Ziglar. When I arrived with my wife, Tammy, I discovered that Zig was hosting the Sunday School class he taught at Prestonwood Baptist Church in Dallas, and that I had been mistaken for a class member.

I shared with Zig what had happened; and he invested over an hour with me personally during that event, giving me a tour of their home, sharing with me his business philosophies and how he researches, and really just mentoring me through some of the mistakes he made and things that worked well for him. He spent more time with me that evening than he did with his other invited guests, which was a blessing I'll remember for the rest of my life. He was a selfless giver, and he truly had a desire to inspire others. He was a huge encourager to me, and I have attempted to repay his generosity by being an encourager for those with whom I have had the pleasure of working.

Half a decade later, I experienced serendipity when I sat across from Zig and his president in first class on a flight to Detroit. I had the privilege of working with Chrysler Corporation to help them become one of the most admired companies in America in the 1990s, and I discovered that Zig and his president were also on their way to Chrysler for an engagement. As I spoke with them on this flight, they were intrigued by my understanding of Chrysler and my ability to get into, and really help, large corporations. Because of this discussion, we went on to co-author a series of video and audio recordings called *Inspire Any Audience*. We stayed connected, played golf, and lunched together from time to time as long as Zig lived, and the man who was his president when I met them on that flight, the late Jim Norman, even became my president ten years later.

I was fortunate to have learned early on in my career that investing in myself would greatly contribute to my success. When I was 22, I attended over 60 seminars. I also learned that books, audios, and videos are powerful tools we all should leverage. I devour them. In fact, this year I have set a goal to listen to 100 best book audios.

Here's one more story. When I was in my 20s, I attended an SMI (Success Motivation Institute) event, and they had an unbelievable special with all their audios on sale for about 80% off. So I bought one of everything! When I told the lady I wanted all of them, she was shocked and asked me to repeat my request, to make sure she had heard me right. I invested about $8,000 in myself right then and there, and that was years ago. I made those recordings part of my library for decades. I even built custom cabinets in my office and catalogued them, and I listened and re-listened to them for years.

I had heard somewhere that if you listen to one audio for 30 minutes a day for a year, you will be an expert on that subject. I thought, "I'll invest an hour a day studying success and results for the rest of my life," and I began that day. Those audios contributed to my designing the life I wanted. I also studied other personal development gurus of that time, including Ken Blanchard, Stephen Covey, Paul Myers (SMI), Zig Ziglar, and Brian Tracy.

Today, there are so many resources at your fingertips: YouTube, Ted Talks, CDs, DVDs, podcasts, and, of course, books. I am a voracious reader, often reading/studying 50 to 100 or more books in a year, and I even have my team recap books so that I can re-read the most important points over and over again and incorporate them into my own life. When I had just graduated from high school, utilizing the resources available to me at that time was what got me intrigued with speed learning, and now teaching other people how to get results faster is one of the biggest value offerings I have.

As a result of these experiences and tools, I began expanding my goals into a file I called the "My Life" file. It not only included goals I wanted to accomplish in the future, it also catalogued personal successes and captured things I had accomplished that I had intentionally set out to do or have or become. The culmination of this became the foundation of *Designing Your Own Life*, which is an expanded version of my original file; and that content is what I want to share with you in these pages so that you may become more intentional in living the life of your dreams and have your best year ever.

How to Use This Book
(So You Get More of What You Want)

I believe that three things really matter when setting goals and getting results: documenting in writing, having visual reminders, and practicing affirming self-talk. *Designing Your Own Life* is divided into three major sections, with the specifics within each section getting progressively more in depth with reflection, filtering, and both short- and long-term goal-setting. It also

> **THREE THINGS REALLY MATTER WHEN SETTING GOALS AND GETTING RESULTS: DOCUMENTING IN WRITING, HAVING VISUAL REMINDERS, AND PRACTICING AFFIRMING SELF-TALK.**

has a common theme of ever-advancing Visionboarding (Resultsboarding) suggestions. And throughout, you will note reminders to keep up positive self-talk (sometimes using written reminders) that reaffirms your values and priorities.

Each section will serve as a blueprint for you personally, designed by you, so that you can live the life of your dreams.

Section 1: Good (Level 1). This level will provide the framework and foundation for *Designing Your Own Life*. In this section you will develop a snapshot of where you are, where you want to go, and what you'll need to get there. It will address who you are personally and allow you to clarify your core beliefs and the things that bring you pleasure, identify your talents, and look at all those things in your life that influence you. Going beyond the personal, you will address the topic of who you are professionally. You will look carefully at your personal brand, your priorities, your career interests, your experiences, and more.

Section 2: Great (Level 2). Once you have a clear picture of who you are and where you want to go personally and professionally, Section 2 will dig deeper into the framework of Section 1 and provide more specifics that will help guide both your personal and professional lives. It will include looking at things in your life you need to do more of or less of, identifying wisdom to live by, clarifying your family priorities, developing personal and family mission statements, and evaluating your Balance Wheel of Life.

Section 3: Mastery (Level 3). Section 3 will take it even further and will include discussions on personal daily standards, timelines, different categories of goals. This section will also look at all the relationships in your life and assist you in both maximizing and assuring congruence between them, including your advisors, mentors, coaches, and others who influence you in positive ways. In this section, you will identify your top talents, document what you are thankful for, and pinpoint the places, events, and experiences that have had an impact on your life to this point…the things that have shaped you. At the end of this section, you will begin detailing your bucket list based on all of the distinctions you'll uncover during this process.

Conclusion

As you begin your work in this book, I want you to know that I don't believe in absolutes. This book is meant as a guide; you do not need to do every exercise in each area of all three sections, and what you DO choose to do can be accomplished in whatever order you find most beneficial and interesting. I recommend that you browse through the entire book before beginning in earnest; and if something really stands out as particularly interesting or valuable for where you are in your life now, go ahead and start there. Similarly, if you determine some of the exercises aren't right for you, or would take up time better spent on other exercises, just skip them. Bounce around. Don't feel obligated to do both the personal and professional exercises; start wherever you want, however you prefer, and enjoy the process. We have even included an expanded Table of Contents in the Appendix at the back of this book that will allow you to rate yourself in each of the areas and identify quickly the areas of highest priority and interest to you. You may want to utilize that as your beginning point, but whatever you do, just get started.

You do not have to complete all the pieces at one time in order to get started with living your more fully designed life. Your life is always a work in progress that continues to be refined as things change and you move on to new priorities. Let me restate that I've been working on my own version of this for many years; it's not as if I sat down one afternoon and wrapped up my life in a couple of hours. I started small, and I started slow; and eventually the way I run my life has turned into the book I am sharing with you. This is about you – you being your best you, you getting everything out of life you have ever dreamed of, and more. Start with Good and work your way through Great and into Mastery at the pace that works for you, understanding that the more you work in Mastery the faster your results will happen.

I revisit and update my version of this often, and so should you. I review it incrementally about once a quarter, and comprehensively once a year. If I get ideas to incorporate during my next review, I note them on my phone in a sort of "brainstorm parking lot" and I encourage you to do the same. Your goal-setting system is a living document that is not, and should not be, static. Your life is dynamic and ever-changing, and your work in this book will be, too.

The main point to remember is that the more intentional you are about specifically designing what you want from life, the better your chances are at getting that life. That's the bottom line.

> YOUR LIFE IS ALWAYS A WORK IN PROGRESS THAT CONTINUES TO BE REFINED AS THINGS CHANGE AND YOU MOVE ON TO NEW PRIORITIES.

"The master in the art of living makes little distinction between his work and his play, his labor and his leisure, his mind and his body, his information and his recreation, his love and his religion. He hardly knows which is which. He simply pursues his vision of excellence at whatever he does, leaving others to decide whether he is working or playing. To him he is always doing both."
-JAMES MICHENER

Contents

Section 1 - Good (Level 1) 23

Introduction 23

Assess Yourself: Six Focus Areas 24
    My Six Focus Areas Assessment 25

Values Tournament 25
    My Values Tournament 26

High Leverage Activities (HLAs) 26
    My High Leverage Activities 28

Strategic Acceleration Frameworks 29
    Personal Framework 29
    Business Framework 32
    Visionboard (Resultsboard) – Level 1 35

Section 1 Summary 36

Section 2 - Great (Level 2) 39

Introduction 39

Who I am Personally 40
    Core Beliefs 40
    Blind Spots 41
    Beliefs to Leverage 43
    Spirituality 44
    Priorities – Pains and Pleasures 45
    Health 46
    Accomplishments 49

Who I am Professionally 51
- Professional Brand 51
- Professional Priorities 55
- Career Interests 57
- Business Strengths 58
- Leadership Effectiveness 59

Life Guidelines 61
- MOLO (More of, Less Of) 61
- Habits to Continue or Eliminate 65
- Spiritual Life 67
- Wisdom to Live By 68
- Sayings and Quotes to Remember 70

Relationships 75
- Family 75
- Spouse/Significant Other 76
- Children 79
- Grandchildren 83
- Extended Family 84
- Friends 85

Goals 86
- Perfect Month 86
- Personal Improvement 88
- Balance Wheel of Life 88
- Visionboard (Resultsboard) – Level 2 91

Section 2 Summary 92

Section 3 - Mastery (Level 3) 93

Introduction 93

Who I am Personally 94
- Talents 95
- Personality Styles 96

 Personal Events of Great Meaning....................100
 Places of Influence................................102
 Personal Daily Standards 103

WHO I AM PROFESSIONALLY..................104
 Business Experiences...............................104
 Ideal Professional Situation 106
 Professional Daily Standards 107

LIFE GUIDELINES................................109
 Thankfulness/Gratitude 109
 Favorite Books of Impact 110

RELATIONSHIPS................................. 116
 Raving Fans..116
 People of Most Influence (POI).....................117
 Advisors...118
 My Life Team 121
 Intentional Congruence 122

GOALS...124
 10 Times as Valuable...............................124
 Likeness 126
 Home Improvement 128
 Timeline of My Projected Life 129
 Travel...130
 Top 100 Life Goals – Bucket List...................132
 Visionboard (Resultsboard) – Level 3...............137

SECTION 3 SUMMARY.........................139

CONCLUSION................................... 141

APPENDICES..................................143

GLOSSARY: TOP TONY JEARY
COINED PHRASES 153

ABOUT TONY JEARY..........................157

What Can Tony Jeary International Do For You? 159

Section 1 - Good (Level 1)

Introduction

This section will focus on getting started. One of the concepts I share with clients I work with is to "go as far as you can see, and then you can see farther." By merely beginning the goal-setting process, and getting things documented, you will be ahead of about 87% of the people who never write them down. Even better, those people who have written goals tend to earn twice as much as those who don't.

> Go as far as you can see, and then you can see further.

The processes in Level 1 will help you begin getting *intentional* results – results that align with the things that actually matter to you. They will be the catalyst to continue going deeper once these are solidified and you have begun to get them ingrained into your thinking and actions.

In this section, we will give you the opportunity to assess yourself and your current status in six key areas. We will walk you through a Values Audit that will allow you to uncover the things that are the most important to you and so that we can align your goals accordingly.

We will begin to develop your *High Leverage Activities* so that you can focus your time on those activities that will bring the greatest results, and we will complete the section by building a Personal and Business Framework from which to build upon in Sections 2 and 3.

Carefully think through those things that are the most important to you, but don't worry about everything being perfect. Remember that goals are ever changing and that this is a living, breathing document that becomes a helpmate for where you spend your time and efforts.

Also take into account that some goals will be accomplished immediately while others may take a lifetime. Having a mixture of both short and long-term goals will give you the satisfaction of completion and also keep you motivated to continue on your journey.

Within these pages, you will find specific examples, instructions on how to complete each item, and blank templates or notes areas so that you can capture your own information.

Assess Yourself: Six Focus Areas

I have identified six strategic areas that matter the most: financial, physical/health, home and family life, education/personal development, social, and spiritual.

I'm a big believer in honestly assessing the current situation before embarking on changes, large or small. Without really getting a grasp of the landscape, you may miss opportunities for improvement or adjustment. And when it comes to my life, and the lives of the individuals I coach, I have identified six strategic areas that matter the most: financial, physical/health, home and family life, education/personal development, social, and spiritual.

Instructions

Where are you in your life today? To get started, assess yourself in the following six areas so you will have a good starting point and get an idea of where you are in each, versus where you want to be. Rate yourself from

1-10 in each, with 10 being the highest.

My Six Focus Areas Assessment

Category	Description	Rating 1-10
Financial	• Is your income where it needs to be? • Is your net worth what you desire and deserve? • Do you have a solid savings/investment strategy? • Is your investment portfolio well-structured? • Are you critically looking at your income and outgo?	
Physical/ Health	• Are your vitals within healthy ranges? • Is your weight appropriate for your structure and height? • Do you have healthy habits relative to intake? • How well do you manage your stress? • Are you getting enough quality rest/sleep?	
Home and Family Life	• Is your relationship with your spouse/significant other supportive, affectionate, and loving? • Are your children happy, well-adjusted, and doing well? • Is your home comfortable and appointed how you want? • Are your relationships with extended family positive?	
Educational/ Personal Development	• Are you reading books both for pleasure and learning? • Do you seek out videos to grow your knowledge? • Are you listening about topics that are relevant? • Are you intentional about experiences to help you grow? • Do you have a team of advisors to help you "do life"?	
Social	• Are you experiencing positive, rewarding social time? • Do you make time to travel and think? • Do the people you surround yourself with have similar values and priorities? • Do you eliminate exposure to negative/toxic people?	
Spiritual	• Do you invest time daily in prayer or meditating? • Are you involved in a worship community? • Do you grow your spiritual knowledge (Bible)? • Are you sharing your faith?	

Values Tournament

Your values are things of great importance to you; they are the things you believe in at your very core. To live an ideal life, and to ensure that your goals are in alignment with the things that are important to you, it is essential that you know clearly what truly matters to you. Living in a way that supports your values will become a part of your happiness and will help guide you in making important choices.

INSTRUCTIONS

What matters most to you? We've identified sixty values below. If you are like most people, a majority of them will resonate with you at some level. However, to get to the core of the things that really matter, circle or highlight the ten that have the highest priority for you.

MY VALUES TOURNAMENT

Affection	Faith	Inspiration	Productivity
Alignment	Fame	Intimacy	Recognition
Altruism	Family	Joy	Respect
Appearance	Financial Security	Knowledge	Results
Appreciated	Freedom	Lifestyle	Routine
Attitude	Friendship	Loyalty	Romance
Cleanliness	Fun	Loved	Security
Congruence	Generosity	Motivation	See the World
Contentment	Genuineness	Openness	Simplicity
Cooperation	Happiness	Organization	Solitude
Creativity	Harmony	Personal Brand	Spiritual Maturity
Education	Health	Personal Improvement	Status
Effectiveness	Honesty	Personal Salvation	Wealth
Efficiency	Humility	Philanthropy	Winning
Fairness	Inner Peace	Power	Wisdom

HIGH LEVERAGE ACTIVITIES (HLAs)

Often, people are moving so fast that they are mostly reacting instead of thoughtfully responding. Sometimes this is necessary; but we believe that the more you can continually find ways to intentionally incorporate the most important actions, the more positive results you will see. *High Leverage Activities* (HLAs) are those activities that if you did more of would give you more of the improved results you want. When your HLAs become

High Leverage Activities (HLAs) are those activities that if you did more of would give you more of the improved results you want.

habits, you will see results. Tracking them by the amount of time spent on each will also help drive them into habits.

There are 168 hours in a week. We sleep approximately 56, and there are 12 for maintenance. That leaves an average of 50 hours for personal and 50 hours for professional activities. We have found that those who are the most successful and have more of what they want invest approximately 70% of their time in their HLAs (35 hours personally, 35 hours professionally).

Instructions

How should you most effectively use the time you have? Use the below examples to think through what applies to you, then write down your own.

Example

High Leverage Activities (Personal)	Average Hours/Week
Exercise 5 times a week (2-3 with a trainer)	5
Date time with spouse	4
Complete daily devotional/meditation	4
Participate in weekly self-development activity	5
Coach and mentor kids	7
Review and update goals	2
Spend time with friends	3
Travel to new places	2
Connect with extended family	3
TOTAL	**35**

High Leverage Activities (Professional)	Average Hours/Week
Make calls to new prospective customers	8
Write up contracts for customers with verbal approval	5
Prepare slides for meetings	2
Follow up on proposals	3
Huddle with staff to ensure clarity of priorities	2
Nourish client relationships	7
Meet with coach	1
Review key emails	4
Think	3
TOTAL	**35**

My High Leverage Activities

High Leverage Activities (Personal)	Average Hours/Week
TOTAL	

High Leverage Activities (Professional)	Average Hours/Week
TOTAL	

Strategic Acceleration Frameworks

The following framework documents are the summary documents that capture the more in-depth information throughout. They are the snapshot view of measuring where you want to go and what you need to do to get there. If you don't want to go quite full-circle on your journey this time around and complete this entire book, then focus ONLY on these Framework documents—one for personal and one for business."

Writing down your goals helps point you in a forward direction. Often, people only document financial goals; but there are many things, of course, that develop an ideal, happy life.

Following are instructions, examples, and templates to guide you as you craft your own Personal and Business Frameworks, which correspond to some of the earlier exercises in this book.

Personal Framework

Instructions

Purpose: Why you do what you do	
Write your purpose statement. This should be inspiring, real, and simple.	
Passion/Happiness: What makes you happy	
List up to 20 words or phrases that describe what you're passionate about and makes you the happiest.	
Values: What's most important to you	
Self	Spouse
List 10 items from the earlier Values Tournament exercise	List 10 items from the earlier Values Tournament for your spouse
Goals: What you want to have, share, experience, give, and become	
Financial	
Physical/Health	
Home and Family Life	Document your high level objectives by area.
Educational/ Personal Development	
Social	
Spiritual	
Other	
Filters: How you filter the world using personality assessments and other tools	
Self	Spouse
List the filters you use and what that means (for example, your personality style).	List the filters your spouse uses and what that means (for example his or her personality style).
Roles: Who you are to others	
Document your roles and purpose to others.	
High Leverage Activities (HLAs): The tasks we perform that directly impact results	
List 5-7 items you need to stay focused on personally. Refer to earlier HLA exercise.	

Example

Purpose: Why you do what you do
The purpose of my life is to live each day happy; in line with my values; helping others win; being a great father, husband, and friend; and giving to, improving, and serving all people.

Passion/Happiness: What makes you happy
Spirituality, wisdom, planning, simplicity, freedom, altruism, health, travel, history, organization, being well dressed, experiencing the outdoors, my kids, serenity, connections, growing, sharing, having fun, success, interacting.

Values: What's most important to you

Self	Spouse
Feel inner peace; be of service to others; be productive; be healthy; experience excitement and adventure; complete tasks; gain wisdom and insight; experience love and affection; be recognized; be punctual.	Feel inner peace; find personal solitude; create an organized and clean environment; spirituality and faith; be of service to others; be appreciated; maintain a structured personal routine and schedule; experience excitement and adventure.

Goals: What you want to have, share, experience, give, and become

Financial	Increase net worth ___% per year; see a positive ROI on investments; grow investment fund by ___%.
Physical/Health	Maintain ideal weight; be disciplined about intake; exercise 60 minutes, 5 days a week (strength, cardio, resistance).
Home and Family Life	Maintain a welcoming, beautifully appointed home; surround myself daily with people who build me up and make me happy.
Educational/Personal Development	Read three books per month; enroll in an online language course; continually grow arsenal of educational tools.
Social	Enjoy as much time as possible with special friends; plan two quality family vacations per year.
Spiritual	Meditate and pray daily; participate in events with like-minded people; continually grow in my faith.
Other	Volunteer one day a week with a non-profit that matters to me; mentor my employees through actions and words.

Filters: How you filter the world using personality assessments and other tools

Self	Spouse
DISC: High D - highly motivated by new challenges, setting and achieving goals, and seeing tangible results. (See our bookstore for this tool.) *Love Language:* Words of Affirmation – value praise, appreciation, reassurance, compliments.	*DISC:* High C – cautious, risk averse, likes to see the facts and weigh options before making decisions. (See our bookstore for this tool.) *Love Language:* Acts of Services – do things specifically to make their life easier and show you care.

Roles: Who you are to others
Spouse, parent, boss, mentor, sibling, volunteer. Positive influence on others, providing clear/frequent communication; opportunities to win; and reliable, solid support.

High Leverage Activities (HLAs): The tasks we perform that directly impact results
Exercise 5 times a week (2-3 with a trainer), date time with spouse, complete daily devotional/meditation, participate in weekly self-development activity, coach and mentor kids, review and update goals, invest time with friends, travel to new places, connect with extended family.

My Personal Framework

Purpose: Why you do what you do

Passion/Happiness: What makes you happy

Values: What's most important to you

Self	Spouse

Goals: What you want to have, share, experience, give, and become

Financial	
Physical/Health	
Home and Family Life	
Educational/ Personal Development	
Social	
Spiritual	
Other	

Filters: How you filter the world using personality assessments and other tools

Self	Spouse

Roles: Who you are to others

High Leverage Activities (HLAs): The tasks we perform that directly impact results

Business Framework

Instructions

Vision: Where you are going

Write your vision statement. A good professional vision is inspiring and realistic.

Mission: Why you exist

Write your mission statement. This should be short and to the point – a statement to be used for yourself or your team/organization.

HLAs: What to focus on

List what you and your team need to do to produce extraordinary results.

Values/Standards: How you conduct yourself/what you believe

Note some of the most important things that you value as a professional and/or a list of professional standards that you and your team agree to.

Mantra: Create an overarching statement that encompasses your values.

Objectives: What you want to accomplish

Yearly: List 5 – 8 goals to be reached each year. A clear objective always begins with an action word, such as "acquire," "communicate," "obtain," "develop," etc.

Strategies: How you will compete and differentiate yourself

Describe the issues to engage in order to reach your objectives.

Actions/Tactics: What needs execution

List the tasks that need to be accomplished to fulfill your strategy and reach your objectives.

CSFs or KPIs: How you measure your success

Detail the metrics and targets that will show movement and results toward your objectives.

"Distractions are a part of our everyday lives. You should know where you are today. You should also know where you are going. There is a gap between where you are and where you're going – which leads you to your HLA's...the things to really focus on."

– Tony Jeary

Example

Vision: Where you are going

Positively impact our clients' results in compressed time-frames our competitors can't match, whereby our global demand consistently exceeds our supply.

Mission: Why you exist

Drive extraordinary results for clients and in return provide exceptional compensation that supports positive quality of life for each contributing team member.

HLAs: What to focus on

- *ATTRACTING strong, qualified business opportunities*
- *DELIVERING great value to our clients*
- *CLARIFYING direction and improving operations*
- *BUILDING our Wisdom Arsenal of processes, best practices, and tools*
- *NOURISHING connections, extending value, and positively communicating with them*

Values/Standards: How you conduct yourself/what you believe

- *Improve constantly through ongoing COEs, personal SWOTs, and MOLO refinements*
- *Keep everything clean and organized to add to our brand and keep us always ready*
- *Make lists constantly to ensure prioritization, accountability, and faster execution*
- *Over-communicate and calculate to ensure efforts are maximized.*
- *Avoid absolutes (words like never, always, can't).*
- *Focus efforts on new flow of business/revenue*
- *Give favors in advance (FIA); share, give, and help others win*
- *Do things now! Operate with a mindset of quick action and speed to completion while using "Production before Perfection" to manage procrastination.*
- *Be proactive in everything: think ahead, prep ahead, do ahead, invoice ahead, deliver ahead, and exceed expectations all around – internally and externally*
- *Take a team approach – overlap, cross-court, encourage, leverage each other's expertise, and together keep all eyes on getting things done and completing results*

Mantra: *Give value; do more than is expected.*

Objectives: What you want to accomplish

Yearly: Gross: $_____; net: $_____; expand IP (complete 2-5 new books/passports)

Strategies: How you will compete and differentiate yourself

Funnel approach using affiliates, books, events, email and direct mail, web, social media

Actions/Tactics: What needs execution

- *Ongoing smart marketing/sales*
- *Sharing constant value with our clients*
- *Growing our connections*

CSFs or KPIs: How you measure your success

- *Net revenue*
- *Gross revenue*
- *Lead flow per week*
- *Business booked in advance*
- *Testimonials from clients*

My Business Framework

Vision: Where you are going

Mission: Why you exist

HLAs: What to focus on

Values/Standards: How you conduct yourself/what you believe

Mantra:

Objectives: What you want to accomplish

Yearly:

Strategies: How you will compete and differentiate yourself

Actions/Tactics: What needs execution

CSFs or KPIs: How you measure your success

Visionboard (Resultsboard) – Level 1

Most people have no clear vision for how they want to live their life. This is why Visionboarding, or what I term "Resultsboarding" (as the process methodology really does create real, tangible results), is so vital to your personal and professional overall success.

As you progress through this book, you can add to your Resultsboard; ideas for Resultsboarding in Great and Mastery will follow in those respective sections. In the meantime, for more information and resources on how to effectively Resultsboard, do a quick web search for "Tony Jeary Results Visionboarding."

Instructions
Keep it simple for now; this is just the first step!

Example
For example, you can print out and post on a cork board:
- Key takeaways of the exercises you've already completed (especially the Frameworks)
- Cutouts of places you want to visit, items you want to attain, or personal changes you want to make
- Your core values
- High Leverage Activities
- Areas you really want to focus on

My Level 1 Resultsboard Ideas

Section 1 Summary

Congratulations! You have taken the first steps toward *Designing Your Own Life* – and created tools that demonstrate what you want for yourself.

You should now have some clarity of things that are important to you and that align with your values. Having completed this section alone can reap huge rewards for you in a year's time. But note that this is not a one-time activity, but a framework and tool to use to continue on your journey, no matter what stage of life you may be in presently.

> THIS IS NOT A ONE-TIME ACTIVITY, BUT A FRAMEWORK AND TOOL TO USE TO CONTINUE ON YOUR JOURNEY.

What was the most eye-opening part of your discovery within this section?

Why was that important to you? Why was it significant?

If you are ready to take things to the next level and go from Good to Great, Section 2 will lead the way.

Section 2 - Great (Level 2)

Introduction

Sometimes the differences between Good and Great are subtle, but those subtleties can yield significant results. The extra effort in dissecting beliefs and differentiators will help you go to the next level.

In Level 2, we will dig further below the surface to uncover things about your core beliefs and discover in greater detail those things that will contribute to your results.

On the personal side, we will look at your core beliefs and spirituality, capture your priorities, uncover the importance of health, and even capture some of your past accomplishments. This is an often overlooked piece of the puzzle when getting a full picture of where you've been and where you want to be. Accomplishments serve as great motivators and reminders that you have already achieved great things and you are capable of achieving even more.

> **Sometimes the differences between Good and Great are subtle, but those subtleties can yield significant results.**

On the professional side, we will look at your personal brand and uncover your professional priorities. We will capture your career interests and strengths. We will share the importance of having mentors as well as being a mentor so that you can learn from those who are already strong and where you want to be.

Beyond that, we will walk through some guidelines that will help you uncover areas to focus more on and less on so that you get more of what you want. This will spill over into habits to continue or eliminate so that you become the best you that you can be. We will dig deeper into relationships and dissect the importance of each type so that you are more keenly aware of their importance and what those around you want for their lives as well.

Furthermore, we will go deeper into specific goals. We will look at what we call the "Perfect Month" and what that looks like to you, identify areas of improvement that will help make you stronger, and honestly look at your overall life balance. And we will continue with the Resultsboarding you hopefully started in the last section.

Get ready to really dig deeper and go from Good to Great!

Who I am Personally

"Be clear on the beliefs that you filter your life by."
- Tony Jeary

What is your belief system? This is a complex question that only you can answer, even though the answer itself might be incredibly simple. When evaluating your personal philosophy, you need to look at your core beliefs, blind spots, beliefs to leverage, spirituality, priorities, health, and accomplishments. This section will help you clarify your personal philosophy and, in turn, allow you to know why you are pursuing the results you seek. The "why" creates an enormous pulling power that I have seen deliver time and time again.

Core Beliefs

Core beliefs are at the core of who you are as a person and the way you filter the world. You have principles that you've acquired and formed through the years. Being aware of these principles strongly affects your results and drives the way you live and operate your life.

Instructions
What do you really want to accomplish? Document 5 – 7 of your core beliefs to get clarity on what you want now and in the future.

Example
- Be in alignment with my personal standards
- Be an extraordinary spouse
- Raise incredible and productive kids
- Live a lifestyle that is inspiring
- Be motivating for others
- Continually learn and grow

My Core Beliefs

BLIND SPOTS
Blind Spots are inaccurate principles, beliefs, distinctions, and perspectives that limit your thinking, actions, and results. Where do Blind Spots come from? We develop them originally from our upbringing and then

through experience. From the moment we are born, we begin to accumulate experiences and we build a filter that categorizes all we do and all we think. That filter through which we see the world also includes a set of principles or rules we believe to be true. Some principles last a lifetime, but others become outdated. A true example of a blind spot would be outdated principles that we've failed to realize are no longer accurate and yet are shaping our life decisions.

Instructions

Do you have Blind Spots? Think about and write out below 3-5 beliefs that are roadblocks to growing, expanding, and achieving more of what you want.

Example
- I am earning as much as I can right now
- I've learned all I need to learn and am fine with my current personal success
- I need to care about only the bottom line
- There's not a lot of value in leveraging the advice/insight of others
- I should focus only on succeeding today and not on building a legacy
- Helping others win isn't a very good use of my time or energy

My Blind Spots

BELIEFS TO LEVERAGE

Core beliefs, which are generally positive (vs. blind spots, or inaccurate beliefs that can have a negative impact), are at the root of who you are as a person and the way you filter the world. You can leverage those core beliefs, which drive the way you live and operate your life. Being aware of your core beliefs strongly affects your results.

Instructions

What beliefs can help you? Think about 3-5 of your beliefs that you can leverage to get better results; then document them below.

Example
- Having and leveraging a highly talented and intentionally built team will help me be extremely effective and accomplish life at the top level
- Making lists greatly impacts my ability to execute and create wins for everyone around me
- Being extremely clear on what I want to experience, share, give, have, and become provides a pulling power for success
- Being intentionally congruent and thoroughly planning every detail eliminates stress and provides quantum execution leaps
- Maintaining and strengthening my relationships with my family and friends motivates me to continually improve and "count my blessings"

My Beliefs to Leverage

SPIRITUALITY

We all have certain spiritual guidelines that we follow, although those guidelines can be vastly different. Some adhere to them precisely; others follow them to a lesser degree. Our spirituality guides the way we think and helps us make decisions. This can sometimes overlap with personal values as well.

Instructions

What areas of your life need changing? Where are you weak? Where are you strong? Examine your life and ask yourself where you are from a spiritual maturity standpoint. Using my example, determine the areas that are important to you, give yourself a rating on where you are now, and list actions to take in order to improve your rating.

Example

Area of Evaluation	Rating	Actions to Take
1. Knowledge of scripture	6	Study more
2. Ministry involvement	8	Give away books and resources
3. Joyful giver	8	Be more creative
4. Relationship with spouse	10	Attend more events together
5. Mentor others	9	Guide more/core group of friends
6. Person, work, and gifts of God	7	Encourage others daily
7. Prayer warrior	7	Team up more
8. Witness	7	Plant seeds
9. Worshiper (private and public)	8	Pray more often
10. Home leader	10	Have family studies/discussions

My Spiritual Assessment

Area of Evaluation	Rating	Actions to Take
1.		
2.		
3.		
4.		
5.		
6.		
7.		
8.		
9.		
10.		

PRIORITIES – PAINS AND PLEASURES

Pain causes stress, and stress causes cortisol to jet into your body. High or prolonged levels of cortisol in the bloodstream have been shown to have negative effects, such as impaired cognitive performance, suppressed thyroid function, blood sugar imbalances, decrease in muscle tissue, higher blood pressure, and increased abdominal fat.

Understanding those things that cause "pain" reactions to you – things that make you uncomfortable or anxious and that you want to avoid – and those things that bring you pleasure will help you become more aware and eliminate negativity as much as possible.

There are huge benefits to understanding the things that cause you pain and focusing on those things that bring positive feelings into your life. When you're happy, your brain is stimulated, and your focus is steadier.

Instructions

What are your pains, and what are your pleasures? Identify your pains to avoid to help you reduce stress and wasted time. Identify your pleasures, and you'll have specific goals that can be reached in small, simple ways – every day.

Example

Pains (To Avoid)	Pleasures (To Have)
• Being around negative people • Consuming sugary and high-fat foods • Spending time in a disorganized house or office • Waiting in lines • Sitting in traffic • Leaving money "on the table" • Mismatched clothes • Dirty cars • Miscommunication	• Surrounding myself with positive people of influence • Dressing well/with style • Living debt-free • Having many friends • Traveling the world • Getting results • Maintaining a healthy, toned body • Enjoying vitals at the top of the charts • Getting results!

My Pains and Pleasures

Pains (To Avoid)	Pleasures (To Have)

Health

Most people get busy with their life and leave health as "less than top priority." We believe health is a big piece to the puzzle of getting what you want. We think it has a direct correlation to your ability to work at peak performance and alertness. Having a strong mind and body directly affects your ability to execute your goals.

> HEALTH IS HOLISTIC – IT IS NOT JUST ABOUT WEIGHT OR EXERCISE OR PHYSICAL AILMENTS.

Health is holistic – it is not just about weight or exercise or physical ailments. It includes mental health, toxins, vitamins, and other specifics, like getting the right amount of sleep. It all works together to help you perform at your peak.

Instructions

How strong are your mind and body? Below are 20 specific areas of opportunity in the area of health that contribute to your overall effectiveness. We featured this in my book Ultimate Health. Rate yourself between 1 and 10 (10 being the highest) in each area, documenting how well you are living at peak performance currently, which will provide insight into future improvements.

My Whole Health Assessment

Category	Description	Rating
Lifestyle	How are you living your life? Managing balance, managing risks, resting, saying "no" enough, and exercising all make up your overall routine. Are your habits supporting health?	
Mental Management	What goes on in our minds truly impacts our health. Assess your own self-talk, your daily attitude, your beliefs about being healthy and not getting sick, and your willingness to release grudges and forgive, while focusing on the positives. Filter the input you receive from sources such as news, media, or even negative people.	
Ultimate Longevity	Do you have a great team of health professionals that know you and guide you? Family doctor? Nutritionist? Dentist? Do you have regular checkups and vaccines? Do your behaviors align with real health?	
Stress Management	Are you managing anxiety? Are you meditating? Relaxing enough? Is your life aligned with your values? Have you set up harmony in your life so things run as smoothly as possible? Is your pace of life contributing to or detracting from your overall well-being?	
Immune System	Your immune system protects you. It detects potential harm and helps your body react. Are you helping yourself? Are you resting at the right time (for example, when you sense your body needs it to ensure you stay well)? Are you maintaining good hygiene; protecting against harmful bacteria; and practicing plain and simple cleanliness, such as washing your hands enough?	
Testing	Early detection is great common sense in today's world of information. How is your discipline on staying current on screenings, blood work reviews, EKGs, MRIs, hormone testing, and urinalysis? There are many things we can do to be proactive. Are you taking advantage of these options?	
Exercise	Physical exercise matters—regular, frequent, and ongoing. Resistance exercise, cardiovascular exercise (aerobics), balance, and stretching all promote a better-operating body.	
Oral	Obviously, it is important to keep your mouth clean. Are you brushing enough? Flossing enough? Going for regular checkups?	
Eyes/Vision	Are you protecting your eyes from sunlight and eating the things that help prevent cataracts later in life? Are you going for regular checkups? Do you wear eye protection when doing certain types of work around the house? All these factors add up to promoting this key component to your body's overall health.	
Toxin Management	What's around you can get in your body through your skin, what you breathe, and what you eat. Toxins are potentially hazardous substances that can place an extra toll on your body, such as forcing your liver and kidneys to work overtime as they filter fluids. Are you protecting yourself like you could or should?	
Hormone Management	A hormone is a chemical released by a cell or a gland in one part of your body that sends out messages that affect cells in other parts of your body. In essence, it's a chemical messenger that transports a signal from one cell to another. Have you tested your chemical balances (estrogen, testosterone, thyroid, DHEA, etc.)? Are you supplementing where you should?	

Vitamins	A vitamin is an organic compound required as a vital nutrient in tiny amounts by an organism. Vitamins help your body function optimally. Are you managing your regular intake, testing so you know, and living daily with the right balances in your body?	
Caloric Management	A calorie is a unit of energy. It is a measure of the energy we generate with every task we do, as well as a measure of the energy delivered by a food we eat. How well do you know your body and how do you balance what you eat versus what you need to perform? Being in tune and knowing this can allow you to make better daily choices and live better!	
Ear, Nose, and Throat	Preventive testing is important for the ear, nose, and throat, the same as for the rest of your body. It is important to protect your hearing and ear canal from foreign objects and loud noises. Are you getting checked regularly?	
Food	Food is any substance consumed to provide nutritional support for your body. It is usually of plant or animal origin, and contains essential nutrients, such as carbohydrates, fats, proteins, vitamins, and minerals. It is what we consume in an effort to produce energy, maintain life, and stimulate growth. How is your balance? How is your mix? Are you eating throughout the day to promote good metabolism? Do you eat slowly and chew well in order to promote good digestion? Do you make healthy choices such as limiting the fried, processed, and high-sugar foods you eat?	
Skin	Your skin is the largest organ in your body. It acts as an external filter and can even provide many clues about the condition of your body internally. Are you protecting it like you should from ultraviolet rays or from harmful chemicals that can get into your body? Do you get full-body skin screenings to detect cancers or other harmful things that need attention in order to ensure your ultimate health? Skin cancer is the most common cancer there is.	
Fluids	Consuming adequate amounts of water is critical to maintaining ultimate health. Do you drink enough water each day? Do you manage your alcohol intake? Do you drink too much soda or other high-sugar drinks?	
Emotions	Emotion is a complex psycho-physiological experience of your state of mind as you interact with internal and external influences. How are your mood, temperament, personality, disposition, and motivation? All these elements matter; all impact the way our bodies perform.	
Sleep	Sleep suspends the sensory activity of nearly all voluntary muscles. It accentuates the growth and rejuvenation of the immune, nervous, skeletal, and muscular systems. Are you getting enough sleep? Is it good sleep?	
Spiritual Wellness	Your spiritual wellness is to a large degree reflective of your worldview. Is it egocentric or others oriented? Would others say you display stress tolerance and adequate marginal reserves for life's challenges? What wisdom do you apply to your life situations in order to achieve spiritual balance, peace, and joy?	

Your Total: _____

Accomplishments

People often fail to capture and celebrate accomplishments, and then they get defeated when they aren't moving forward as quickly as they had hoped. Capturing accomplishments serves as inspiration and motivation to continue moving forward. An accomplishment is a work or act completed and valued by yourself or others. If you examine your accomplishments and find a trend, you'll see that you can very quickly and easily validate your values as well. It is also an excellent way to appreciate the blessings you have in your life.

Instructions

What have you accomplished? Complete your own inventory so that you can use past accomplishments to motivate your future success.

Example

Things I've Seen

Australia, Italy, Greece, Rocky Mountains, South Africa, Korea, Amsterdam windmills, Spain, Cabo San Lucas, most Caribbean Islands, Japan, Taiwan, Middle East, Vienna, World Series, Rio Copa Cabana, Germany, Fisher Island, NASA, Stingray City, NY Stock Exchange (Commodities Floor), MGM Studios, Disney World, Epcot Center

Things I've Experienced

Swam with sharks, sting rays, and dolphins; Oasis (largest cruise ship); kids to NYC; at 8, kids published a book; Hot Springs; given away a car; NY Subway; survived a tornado, electric shock, and quicksand; country club memberships; bought parents' home; auctioneered; built dozens of homes' sailed on yachts around the globe; skied backwards; flown an airplane; flown in a helicopter

Things I've Shared

Taking kids to new country every year they've been alive, extraordinary parties with family (birthdays, proms, graduations), building a great Resultsboard with family, vacations with friends and kids' friends, seeing clients excel financially and celebrating their successes, living in my dream home, mentoring multiple Interns, meeting extraordinary people with others, business success

Things I've Become
Respected authority, mentor, caring husband and father, encourager, advocate for health, business success, well-respected community volunteer

Things I Have (or Have Had)
Top notch home office, well-appointed home, many connections, luxury cars, bank stock, self-owned and successful business, gold/platinum/black credit cards, a swimming pool, a boat, purebred dog

My Accomplishments

Things I've Seen

Things I've Experienced

Things I've Shared

Things I've Become

Things I Have (or Have Had)

Who I Am Professionally

Professional Brand

Companies spend a lot of money and effort to build their brands. Building a brand is important because it communicates who you are professionally to prospects and customers. While you can certainly be judged partly by the brand of the company you represent, having your own brand is the way others perceive you individually. In order for people to perceive you the way you want them to and build the brand you want to be known for, it is important to be conscious about what you want that to be.

> A TRUE PROFESSIONAL SHOULD BE ABSOLUTELY CLEAR ON WHO THEY ARE AND WHAT THEY STAND FOR; AND, OF COURSE, THEY CAN AND SHOULD COMMUNICATE THIS IN ALL THE ASPECTS OF THEIR LIFE.

A true professional should be absolutely clear on who they are and what they stand for; and, of course, they can and should communicate this in all the aspects of their life. The matrix below can act as a foundation to speed up the process of clarifying your brand.

Instructions

Element	Description
Brand Description	10-word phrase that summarizes the essence of my brand positioning (the following items)
Core Value Proposition	Core characteristics that are valuable to my effectiveness
Business Priorities	Parameters and priorities for how I operate on a daily basis
I am	Characteristics that describe me
I am Not	Characteristics that do **not** describe me
Uniqueness	What truly makes me unique and separates me
Packaging	Tools, expertise, image, etc. to leverage
Visual Image	Physical image/appearance
Mission Statement	What drives my decisions
Brand Power	The "thrust" behind my reputation
Tagline	Benefit-driven, descriptive declaration (said often)
Positioning	Role(s) within the market/organization
Business Motto	Statement of approach to business life
What People Think Of Me	My perception of how I am perceived
What People Are Missing	My beliefs on what others misunderstand about me
Prized Workplace Attributes	The attributes I possess that my organization values
Passions	What I am passionate about
Top 4 Marketing Tools	Top tools and tactics to leverage
My Audience/Prospect	Who I most want to impact
External Barriers	Real world roadblocks
Internal Barriers	Self-imposed roadblocks

Example

Element	Details
Brand Description	Coach to the world's top CEOs and high achievers, known as The RESULTS Guy™
Core Value Proposition	Speed alignment; clarity, focus, and execution; accelerated results methodology
Business Priorities	Deliver 90% of work from home office; be a trusted advisor; enjoy stress-free living
I am	Strategic, disciplined, hardworking, an expert, organized, a fast thinker, energetic, entertaining
I am Not	Fake, lazy, dishonest
Uniqueness	Speed in delivering results, private studio facility, results authority, author of dozens of books
Packaging	Time efficient, experienced team, vast life experience, immense body of knowledge and resource library
Visual Image	Stylish, sharp, healthy, fit
Mission Statement	My business supports my lifestyle
Brand Power	Authority (through books and celebrity and well-known clients)
Tagline	"Strategic Acceleration through Clarity, Focus, and Execution"
Positioning	Results strategist, thought leader, author
Business Motto	Give value; do more than is expected.
What People Think Of Me	Committed, results-focused
What People Are Missing	True value of what we can do (return on investment); speed of execution
Prized Workplace Attributes	Accomplishment, dependability, quick thinking, organization, speed, track record
Passions	Achieving positive results; building and maintaining respectable reputation
Top 4 Marketing Tools	Website, videos (YouTube), promoters, social media
My Audience/Prospect	Mega-achievers, corporate C-level execs, speaker/author/expert types
External Barriers	Time
Internal Barriers	Balancing work and family – ensuring wins for both

My Professional Branding Matrix

Element	Details
Brand Description	
Core Value Proposition	
Business Priorities	
I am	
I am Not	
Uniqueness	
Packaging	
Visual Image	
Mission Statement	
Brand Power	
Tagline	
Positioning	
Business Motto	
What People Think Of Me	
What People Are Missing	
Prized Workplace Attributes	
Passions	
Top 4 Marketing Tools	
My Audience/Prospect	
External Barriers	
Internal Barriers	

Professional Priorities

What are your professional priorities? What type of environment do you really enjoy working in? What suits you best and helps you maximize your talent and personal style? What helps you feel and operate at your maximum effectiveness? Take a step back and examine this to make sure you put yourself in an environment that sets you up to succeed!

Instructions

What is your ideal environment? Think about ways to leverage your talent, your desired amount of travel, type of team members, etc. that help make you shine. These priorities may change over time, and some things will be 1 year, 3 years, or even 5 years away. Understanding these things will help you better focus on creating that perfect situation for yourself and working in your desired areas. Below, document the work environment qualities you desire and the specifics needed to reach that desire.

Example

Work Environment Qualities	Specifics to Reach Desire
1. Maintenance free	Documented systems and processes
2. Flexible hours	Ensures margin time
3. Honest feedback	Be real and expect the same from others
4. Clean and organized	Documented visual standards guides
5. Remits quickly	Ensure solid payment pipeline
6. Capitalize on my talents	Choose the right engagements
7. Education	Be around people I can learn from
8. Travel	Book engagements in desirable locations
9. Meet interesting people	Select interesting experiences
10. In my home	Leverage the setup
11. Occasionally outside	Schedule things outside when can
12. Valued	Pick extraordinary clients
13. Appreciated	Pick extraordinary clients
14. Positive team	Contract the right people and help them win in life
15. Respected clients	Market to target market

My Professional Priorities

Work Environment Qualities	Specifics to Reach Desire
1.	
2.	
3.	
4.	
5.	
6.	
7.	
8.	
9.	
10.	
11.	
12.	
13.	
14.	
15.	

Career Interests

Many people sit back and let their careers happen *to* them, while others move forward and make their careers happen *for* them. When we identify areas of interest in our lives and careers, we tend to flow toward them rather than drift aimlessly away from them. What are some career areas you are truly interested in? Are there avenues that you would really like to pursue and believe that you would likely succeed at?

Instructions

What keeps you inspired? Think about and then document things that keep you inspired and motivated and things that really interest you. These interests can be types of career positions, or characteristics like business growth, problem-solving, fast results, etc. Make sure they are things that paint a picture of your ideal situation. The sky's the limit – there are no self-imposed limitations.

Example

Seeing clients excel financially and celebrating their successes, working in my dream environment, mentoring multiple interns and employees, meeting extraordinary people

My Career Interests

BUSINESS STRENGTHS

Many people mistake skill for talent. Some of the most successful and skilled individuals are not necessarily "talented," but are committed to learning and acquiring a distinction or knowledge that propels them to effective performance.

Instructions

What skills do you have now? What skills do you want to acquire? Using the below examples as a guide, document your own.

Example

Current Business Strengths — *Organizing, getting results faster, marketing, managing, planning, working with numbers, focusing, speaking, training, negotiating, managing time*

Desired Business Strengths — *Networking, facilitating, clarifying, team building, managing life*

My Business Strengths

Current Business Strengths

Desired Business Strengths

LEADERSHIP EFFECTIVENESS

Over the past two decades, I have been blessed to coach (and learn from!) some of the world's most influential and successful individuals. Based on this exposure, I have learned that those who get the best results have distinctions in five strategic areas: executive focus and clarity, personal development and strength in decision making, presentation and communication skills, leading a strong team, and people power. From there, I created an assessment that has 25 best practices that, when leveraged, create wins over and over again.

Instructions

How impactful are you as a leader? Assess how well you are currently leveraging the below best practices. Rate yourself from 1-4 in each with 4 being the highest.

> I HAVE LEARNED THAT THOSE WHO GET THE BEST RESULTS HAVE DISTINCTIONS IN FIVE STRATEGIC AREAS: EXECUTIVE FOCUS AND CLARITY, PERSONAL DEVELOPMENT AND STRENGTH IN DECISION MAKING, PRESENTATION AND COMMUNICATION SKILLS, LEADING A STRONG TEAM, AND PEOPLE POWER.

	Executive Focus and Clarity	Rating
1.	**Strategic Plan**: Creating and refining a powerful and well thought-out plan tied to a simple, well thought-out vision	
2.	**Vision Model/Tools**: Using cascading tool(s) that complement your vision and make sharing easy and efficient	
3.	**SWOT/MOLO**: Evaluating your strengths and weaknesses and what you want to do more of and less of, two or three times a year	
4.	**Benchmarking**: Looking at best practices, then modeling part or all to get results others have accomplished	
5.	**Competitive Comparison Matrix**: Knowing your competition, sharing with your team all strengths, weaknesses, trends, sweet spots, etc.	
	Personal Development and Strength in Decision Making	
6.	**Strategic Presence**: Taking a strategic approach to your Professional Brand and communicating it to investors, other departments, and customers	
7.	**Health/Energy Management**: Managing diet, timing, and stress to operate at peak performance for all opportunities	
8.	**Feeding Your Mind**: Constantly innovating, growing, and learning (read, listen, and be coached to consistently model self-improvement for others)	
9.	**Managing HLAs**: Understanding prioritization and doing what matters most to see real results	
10.	**Reality vs. Numbers**: Measuring successes and opportunities using a scorecard that captures CSFs or KPIs	
	Presentation and Communication Skills	
11.	**Meeting Effectiveness**: Ensuring all meeting invites and meetings have strong objectives, a good agenda, the right people, and clear actions	
12.	**Presentation Ready**: Understanding your Presentation Universe so you're clear on all your most impactful presentations and you're ready to deliver	
13.	**Personality Profile**: Using personality profiling (i.e., DISC) when hiring, motivating, negotiating, etc.	
14.	**Information Management**: Getting the information you need quickly and on a regular basis so that you're in a strong position to make better decisions	
15.	**Team Huddles**: Calibrating your team to synchronizing focus and clarity of priorities, either by phone or in person	
	Leading a Strong Team	
16.	**Performance Standards**: Develop the rules of engagement for yourself and those around you to ensure expectations are met	
17.	**Mentoring**: Truly supporting those you lead and creating better bench strength through coaching and the sharing of ideas	
18.	**People of Influence (POI)**: Interfacing consistently with those who have the biggest influence on your objectives	
19.	**Advisors**: Nurturing a team of individuals (coach, mentors, etc.) that help guide, stimulate, and bring fresh ideas and perspectives	
20.	**Culture**: Building a team synergy based on continual improvement, trust, accountability, and open communication	
	People Power	
21.	**Assistant Effectiveness**: Leveraging your personal support staff to help you be Presentation Ready, organized, and ready to win	
22.	**Time Saving Team**: Utilizing a team (assistant, driver, researcher, travel agent, etc.) who know you well and save your time and energy	
23.	**Networking/Connections**: Having a system for building and nourishing new and existing contacts	
24.	**Social Capital**: Doing positive things for people in your world in advance in order to have a "bank account" to request favors and actions	
25.	**Stuff Management**: Handling inflow of information and physical items, sorting, organizing, retrieving, and archiving	

Your Total: _____

Life Guidelines

Guidelines are all about gaining clarity on the way that you operate (or want to operate) in life. There are many times where guidelines help us execute more effectively and operate in the manner we want. Your guidelines should be formed based how you spend your time (and maybe should NOT spend it); what habits are positive or negative; your spiritual strengths; and what wisdom/advice from others really matters, reinforces your vision and ultimately impacts results.

MOLO (More of, Less Of)

MOLO stands for More Of, Less Of. It's about stepping back and evaluating what we need to do More Of to have more of what we want, or Less Of by eliminating or delegating things that don't contribute to results.

> MOLO STANDS FOR MORE OF, LESS OF. IT'S ABOUT STEPPING BACK AND EVALUATING WHAT WE NEED TO DO MORE OF TO HAVE MORE OF WHAT WE WANT, OR LESS OF BY ELIMINATING OR DELEGATING THINGS THAT DON'T CONTRIBUTE TO RESULTS.

Instructions

How should you REALLY be spending your time? Think about how and why doing specific things differently can dramatically change your outcomes.

Example – Personal MOLO

What Do I Need To Do More Of?	
What	**Why**
Hold family/staff meetings/events	Gain better focus/priorities
Save/invest more money (__% of gross)	Show responsibility
More time with family	Nourish our special relationship
Dates and 1:1 time with spouse	Keep our marriage strong
Slow down/smell the roses more	Enjoy results of hard work
What Do I Need To Do Less Of?	
What	**Why**
Maintenance activities	Not fun; time better spent
Eating unhealthy foods	Continue to improve health
Personal errands	Better utilize my time and leverage staff
Focus on the negative	Positivity is a pulling power
Interact with toxic people	Drains energy

Example – Professional MOLO

What Do I Need To Do More Of?	
What	**Why**
Time in High Leverage Activities (HLAs)	Maximize time and value for results
Consistent huddles with assistant	Manage time efficiently
Model leadership characteristics	Cascade best practices/better lead
Be organized	Creates efficiency
Nurture relationships with clients	Establish good connections
What Do I Need To Do Less Of?	
What	**Why**
Take on clients that aren't ideal	Not a High Leverage Activity
Personal research	Not best use of time
Last-minute prep	Stress
Unnecessary meetings	Sucks up too much time
Lower level activities	Need to save my time and leverage staff

My Personal MOLO

What Do I Need To Do More Of?	
What	**Why**

What Do I Need To Do Less Of?	
What	**Why**

My Professional MOLO

What Do I Need To Do More Of?	
What	Why

What Do I Need To Do Less Of?	
What	Why

HABITS TO CONTINUE OR ELIMINATE

Habits are those things you do regularly – good or bad – that form a consistent pattern of how you operate in life.

Instructions

Are your current habits producing all the results you really want? Take a moment to list your habits in each of the major roles you play in life and rate yourself on a scale of 1-10 (10 being highest).

Example

Role	Spouse	Rating	xx
Positive Habits to Maintain	*Sharing same beliefs, helping them win, knowing what they care about, appreciating them verbally, being supportive of them*		
Negative Habits to Eliminate	*Being inflexible, taking for granted, not spending enough quality time, not communicating enough using their Love Language*		

Role	Child(ren)	Rating	xx
Positive Habits to Maintain	*Showing respect, spending time doing things they like to do, listening more, asking their counsel, telling them they are loved*		
Negative Habits to Eliminate	*Taking for granted, dismissing their ideas, keeping important things from them, being critical*		

Role	Parent(s)	Rating	xx
Positive Habits to Maintain	*Encouraging them, spending time with them, telling them you love them, supporting things that matter to them*		
Negative Habits to Eliminate	*Being critical, putting them off until another time, being too busy, not asking for counsel*		

Role	Career Position	Rating	xx
Positive Habits to Maintain	*Being organized and efficient, serving others, showing open-mindedness, modeling self-discipline, trusting others*		
Negative Habits to Eliminate	*Having arguments, allowing lack of completion, procrastinating, not delegating more (letting go)*		

My Habits

Role	Spouse	Rating
Positive Habits to Maintain		
Negative Habits to Eliminate		

Role	Child(ren)	Rating
Positive Habits to Maintain		
Negative Habits to Eliminate		

Role	Parent(s)	Rating
Positive Habits to Maintain		
Negative Habits to Eliminate		

Role	Career Position	Rating
Positive Habits to Maintain		
Negative Habits to Eliminate		

Role	Other:	Rating
Positive Habits to Maintain		
Negative Habits to Eliminate		

Spiritual Life

The most important part of ANY building, regardless of how beautiful or functional it is, or its size, is the foundation. In life, I have found that nurturing a commitment to spiritual maturity has affected my results, because I have a strong base of guidelines on which to make decisions and better form my Belief Window. These guidelines will weather any storm.

Instructions

What guidelines or foundation are you building your life upon? What spiritual guidelines are important to you? Truly contemplate the foundation your life is built upon; then list the guidelines here.

Example

Be humble, be a servant, have character, be a builder, be forgiving, be faithful, set an example, give things away (share), don't be attached to material things, reject anything that brings addiction, make things that last (systems), remember your environment

My Spiritual Guidelines

Wisdom to Live By

For all of us, there are specific things or ideas we've picked up that have helped us make our professional lives better. These are principles that we incorporate into the way we do business on a regular basis. Keeping a list of these will help utilize best practices to continually grow and execute for results.

Instructions

Do you leverage the wisdom of others? I wrote a book called *Business Ground Rules* with Peter Thomas (available on my website at http://www.tonyjeary.com/bookstore) that lists 100 lessons for success. They are in 12 separate categories: Thinking, Clarity, Time, Strategy, Focus, Brand, Leadership, People, Money, Wealth, Execution, and Health. Check the below lessons that resonate most with you.

My Wisdom to Live By

Thinking	
Live life on purpose	
Have fun and make money	
Eliminate Blind Spots from your Belief Window – be open-minded	
Select mentors carefully and have them help you think smart	
Look deep – there's a pony in there somewhere (find what is hard to see)	
Do what wealthy people do; think how wealthy people think	
Avoid negative thoughts	
Value your daily solitude	
Get a coach	
Deploy the AMC™ (attitude, motivation, commitment) test in your business	
Ask your coaches and mentors for their recommended reading lists	
Foster joy, entertainment, and inspiration	
Sharpen your sword and precise communication	
Help others win	
Express gratitude	
Beware of King Arthur's Disease – don't get over-confident and ignore risk	
Avoid FUD (fear, uncertainty, doubt) – FUD creates mediocrity	
Give back	
Lead a no-excuses culture	
Clarity	
Clarity: Get it and use it	
Align goals with your values	
You can't get where you're going without a plan	
Make a life list	
Design your own life	
Utilize the power of visualization	
Pause to reflect	
Develop a Likeness Matrix – who you want to be like for different reasons	

Time
- Say "no" often
- Manage time – don't let time manage you
- MOLO your life and business often (do More Of, Less Of)
- Create Elegant Solutions (one thing that serves multiple purposes)
- Understand positive and negative procrastination

Strategy
- Be intentional about everything
- Establish the rules before you start the game
- Use the tools that give you leverage
- Initially structure a partnership or business properly
- Watch for warning signs
- Know the rules of negotiation
- Stay competitive
- Reward yourself often to create inspiration and motivation
- Move from Great to Mastery in all you do
- Live in solutions – be strategic versus tactical
- Ask questions to get leverage
- Build your future through delayed gratification
- Leverage strategic coaching
- Benchmark for best practices

Focus
- Understand and Study the Concept of High Leverage Activities (HLAs)
- Focus is the opposite of distraction
- Aim for 87 percent
- Maintain your personal agenda in hard times
- Appreciate (and invest time in) what you want more of

Brand
- Be known for something
- Brand yourself
- Develop a memorable, influential persona
- Be real – people appreciate transparency
- Your body language and appearance impact your success
- Do favors in advance (and then people will do favors for you)
- Be a connector
- Be interested, not just interesting
- Ensure strategic alignment between your branding, marketing, and sales
- Be presentation ready

Leadership
- Freedom comes from absolute discipline
- Develop perseverance
- Live by documented personal standards
- Channel your emotions and control your ego
- Be a person of influence
- Delegate a lot more
- Utilize personality profiling to better understand yourself and others
- Support a high-energy culture

People
- Surround yourself with successful, positive people
- Create and nourish a Life Team
- Jockeys are more important than the horses
- You can't do a good deal with a bad guy
- Build relationships and help others win
- Listen up – be a great listener if you want to be successful
- Focus on people of influence

Money	
Win big (or at least lose small)	
Establish a relationship with a banker who likes you	
Put your understanding of a deal in writing	
Pay average salaries and higher bonuses (incentivize)	
Keep your will current	
Pay all small suppliers on time	
Make others feel significant	
Wealth	
Be financially strong	
Don't fall in love with an asset	
Be a risk assessor, not a risk taker	
Continually upgrade the size of your deals	
Inspect before your acquire	
Execution	
Speed matters – accelerate results	
Have a "get it done now" mindset	
Practice "Production before Perfection" – get started and polish later	
Execute with accountability	
Measure everything – measurement matters	
Focus on results versus activity	
Work the plan; utilize a scorecard	
Health	
Do business in places you consider enjoyable – it will reduce stress	
Live healthy	
Maintain a strong mental mindset	
Live ultimate longevity	
Manage stress – stress affects everything	

SAYINGS AND QUOTES TO REMEMBER

For years I've been inspired by certain phrases (words carefully put together that create thoughts that really matter). Everyone has heard a saying or two (or, in my case, hundreds!) that resonate with where your life is going, and what you want to be. But storing them all mentally can be a real task. I have found that documenting and regularly reviewing the sayings and quotes that matter most to me keep me inspired.

Instructions

What personal sayings and quotes inspire and motivate you to be your best? Accumulate them and continuously add to – and review – the list. Below are some examples (check the ones that resonate the most) and an area for you to add your own. You can even print out your favorites to put in your wallet or post where you can often be inspired (such as your Resultsboard).

Example

Sayings and Quotes to Remember	
Be both strategic and intentional about every single thing you do.	
Love what you do AND do what you love.	
Budget for strategy first; it matters the most.	
Get clear on what you want to have, share, experience, and perhaps most importantly, what you want to become.	
The best way to achieve extraordinary results is to become intentional about being strategic in all areas of your life.	
Remember "clarity" pulls you toward the results you envision.	
You can live a physical age that is less than your chronological age; it starts with clarity of what you want.	
Become a person who is willing to give, share, and create value for others.	
Go through life with well thought-out and documented values that you can live your life by, and then align your goals and time accordingly.	
Have a solution-oriented attitude and a "how do we?" vs. a "why?" mindset.	
It's important to choose Life Team Members whose gifts and talents complement your own, and make sure you constantly find ways to show them appreciation.	
It's not about the grades you make as much as it is about the hands you shake - cherish and build relationships.	
Know what really, really makes you happy; then build a life around it.	
No single skill or habit has a more powerful impact on results than the ability to eliminate distractions and focus on High Leverage Activities (HLAs).	
The belief that greatness already exists becomes the enemy of mastery.	
If you choose to live in solutions, the world eagerly awaits your dreams and provides every tool and opportunity you need to turn them into reality.	
There is an awesome power in committing your goals to writing — yet very few people can actually show you their written goals. Be one of the few.	
Your goals should be absolutely congruent with your values. It starts with what you want to accomplish.	
Have written goals all around you (on your closet doors, phones, computers, walls, etc.); clarify what you really want.	
If the results you've been getting have not been what you expect and want, you need to change the way you THINK so you can change your results.	
Focus is a thinking skill acquired as a result of mental discipline.	

My Sayings and Quotes to Remember

Sayings and Quotes to Remember
1.
2.
3.
4.
5.
6.
7.
8.
9.
10.

Sayings and Quotes to Remember

11.

12.

13.

14.

15.

16.

17.

18.

19.

20.

Sayings and Quotes to Remember

21.

22.

23.

24.

25.

26.

27.

28.

29.

30.

Relationships

When we think about relationships, we often tend to lump all relationships into one category. However, there are very distinctly different relationships in your life that contribute to your overall success and happiness. It is important to determine what each relationship needs from you and what you need from them in order to keep them strong. For the purpose of this section, we will primarily be looking at the different relationships in your personal life – family, spouse, significant other, children/grandchildren, extended family, and friends.

> AS A FAMILY, IT IS IMPORTANT TO COMMUNICATE TOGETHER AND DISCUSS WHO YOU WANT TO BE AS A FAMILY.

Family

As a family, it is important to communicate together and discuss who you want to be as a family. It promotes unity with your spouse and children as well as gives operating standards. Having a family mission statement and list of commitments ensures your family operates intentionally versus accidentally. It also reinforces things that are important to you as a unit.

Instructions

Who are you as a family? Together with your family, write your mission statement as well as things you commit to doing together.

Example

Family Mission Statement	*As a family, we will always support each other as a team.*
We commit to doing together these 5 things as much as possible:	1. Playing and having fun 2. Worshipping God 3. Teaching one another 4. Exercising 5. Helping others
We will show everyone, including ourselves, these 5 qualities all the time:	1. Sharing 2. Supporting 3. Loving each other 4. Being thankful 5. Being nice

My Family Mission Statement and Commitments

Family Mission Statement	
We commit to doing together these 5 things as much as possible:	1. 2. 3. 4. 5.
We will show everyone, including ourselves, these 5 qualities all the time:	1. 2. 3. 4. 5.

Spouse/Significant Other

Your spouse or significant other should be the most important personal relationship you have, outside of perhaps your spiritual one. Continuing to place ongoing importance on it is a great way to ensure it stays healthy and doesn't get taken for granted.

This relationship should be very intentional. I have found one of the best ways to keep communication flowing and make this relationship a priority is to "date" your spouse on a regular basis. It is even great for your children to see the importance you place on this relationship and to live out for them what a healthy relationship looks like.

> YOUR SPOUSE OR SIGNIFICANT OTHER SHOULD BE THE MOST IMPORTANT PERSONAL RELATIONSHIP YOU HAVE, OUTSIDE OF PERHAPS YOUR SPIRITUAL ONE.

Another thing most people don't consider is proactively seeking counselors and/or mentors as a couple, even when things are going well. This is an excellent way to get wisdom to maintain a strong relationship and learn from other professionals or couples who have gone through some of the same issues you may be facing.

Instructions

What does (or should) your relationship look like? If you aren't yet married, I encourage you to think about the qualities that are important to you in a future mate and write them down. When you find that person, make sure they have the majority of those qualities instead of settling for something less than what is important to you. When I married my wife over 25 years ago, she had 21 of the 24 qualities I wanted in a spouse.

In addition, as you're defining how to have the best relationship possible, there should be things you both want to do personally, including understanding your spouse's needs more clearly. Use the example below, create your own list, and then mark the ones on each side that are the most important to you and to your spouse. Focus on those and see how your relationship will flourish.

Example

Myself	Spouse	Characteristic
✓	✓	Honesty and openness
✓	✓	Admiration
✓	✓	Family time (family priority)
✓	✓	Attractiveness
✓	✓	Intimacy
✓	✓	Affection
✓	✓	Domestic support
✓	✓	Communication
✓	✓	Leadership
✓	✓	Financial security
✓	✓	Kindness/thoughtfulness
✓	✓	Attention
✓	✓	Loves travel
✓	✓	Supportive
✓	✓	Strong spiritually
✓	✓	Loyalty
✓	✓	Value independence as well as togetherness

My Valued Characteristics

Myself	Spouse	Characteristic

CHILDREN

Crafting an Intentional Family Life

To have a highly successful family, it is important to be intentional about your family life. Parents who see tangible, positive results for their kids set them up to win, help them visualize, provide and model values, help them create their own brand, create meaningful discussions, make and relive memories, and teach them cool things.

> **TO HAVE A HIGHLY SUCCESSFUL FAMILY, IT IS IMPORTANT TO BE INTENTIONAL ABOUT YOUR FAMILY LIFE.**

Instructions

What will you do as parents? Check the items below (from my book, Strategic Parenting) that resonate with you, and then commit to enacting them.

Set Your Kids Up To Win	
Expect the best of your kids and then leverage embedded messages	
Genuinely compliment and appreciate ideal behavior	
Allow your kids to be kids	
Carefully guide your kids to choose the right friends	
Find and support what your kids excel in	
Hire coaches for all angles	
Encourage exploring the world (including the U.S.) at any age	
Give your kids an opportunity to make choices for themselves at a young age	
Settle in a good neighborhood with great neighbors	
Be fair and impartial with your kids	
Eliminate the need for your kid's potential spouse to compete with you	
Build a resume with college binders	
Teach them to build relationships: teachers now, business relationships in the future	
Teach them to understand and respect money	
Explain the differences between competing and winning	
Help Your Kids To Visualize	
Use imagination in dreaming and goal-setting	
Put goals everywhere	
Visualize goals with a family Resultsboard	
Help them define the right kind of spouse	

Model Values For Your Kids	
God matters; make worship a big part of your lives	
Remind them that love trumps everything	
Build great relationships: "It's not the grades you make, but the hands you shake"	
Nourish lifelong friendships	
Let your kids observe your behavior and decision-making	
Teach humility by actions, not words	
Serve, respect, and compliment others	
Pay it forward in reverse; do favors in advance	
Encourage respect for property	
Live a healthy lifestyle	
Teach them that exercising your body also exercises your mind	
Nurture lifelong studying and learning	
Help them prep and organize for school and life each and every day	
Move from parenting to mentoring at the right time	
Show them how to help others win	
Help Your Kids Create Their Own Brand	
Show them how to take responsibility for creating their own brand	
Remember to make joy a part of your brand	
Teach them how building relationships helps build your brand	
Create Meaningful Family Discussions	
Discuss good decision-making	
Leverage games and fun at meals	
Be open about finances, people, and feelings	
Conduct "What did your learn?" discussions (i.e., after a church service or any event); then discuss how it applies and works and can be used, utilized, etc.	
Make And Relive Memories	
Keep things fun!	
Memorialize trips with posters	
Keep "best of best" binders	
Create family video albums	
Provide Models For Your Kids	
Show them the 5 Love Languages	
Explain the Cash Flow Quadrant	
Explain how money works	
Leverage personality styles (DISC)	
Show the importance of learning vs. grades	
Help them play the SAT game	
Show them the difference in a career vs. a job	
Cool Things To Teach Your Kids	
Teach that presenting is a big part of life	
Show them the importance of shaking hands (the ultimate presentation)	
Instill skills they can use forever	
Help them publish books and apps	
Train them to use the newest technology	
Help them clarify their values	
Expand their knowledge	

Ongoing To-Do's	
Take lots of pictures	
Take pictures of your kids' friends (and do something special with them)	
Build an album each year	
Create and maintain a Resultsboard	
Travel to different countries and explore the U.S.	
Brag about your kids strategically	
Be strategic about how you label your kids	
Give trust and show them how to earn it	
Send emails to your kids' teachers and administrative staff	
Hang around with other parents, but choose carefully	
Leverage Facebook and other social media	
Help your kids learn to do new things	
Provide safety and security	
Expose your kids to cool events	
Say "wow, that's a good idea!" a lot (then compliment the activity, task, action, etc.)	
Always make your kids feel welcome in your office	
Create special memories together	
Create unique fun times for bonding	
Encourage every day in every way	
Help your kids build their strengths	
Trust your kids and give them responsibility	

Guiding Your Children's Goals

As your kids grow, teach them to appreciate the power of goals and talk to them about goals; set goals for them as well. Create Resultsboards with them so they can see the things they are going toward. Help them together and review them often.

Instructions

What will we encourage our children to accomplish and become? Below are examples of the types of things to include, but the sky's the limit. Think outside the box – have your kids dream big. Complete for each child and expand the list if needed.

Example

Name:	Jennifer	Date of Birth:	2/12/2000
Love and respect parents, live healthy (food, exercise), understand and be a living example of a person who lives out integrity, marry a person who will love and cherish me, have a serving attitude, join the right crowds, improve computer and technical skills, increase vocabulary, travel to different places and countries, have diverse experiences, be involved in sports or extracurricular activities, be a great friend, eat healthy foods			

My Kids' Goals

Name:		Date of Birth:	

Name:		Date of Birth:	

Name:		Date of Birth:	

GRANDCHILDREN

Going through the same exercises with your grandchildren (which could also include your children in the discussion) can create lasting bonds and will add to the legacy you leave for them. Be open to answering their questions about your relationships and giving them advice.

Instructions

For your grandchildren, we suggest you go through the same process, as appropriate, as you did with your kids to determine ways you can positively contribute to their lives.

My Grandchildren's Goals

Name:	Date of Birth:

Name:	Date of Birth:

Name:	Date of Birth:

EXTENDED FAMILY

For most of us, there are extended family in our lives, near or far, that we need to consider in our overall life picture. Below, make a list of those other important people and what the priorities are for each (parents, grandparents, siblings, cousins, nieces and nephews, etc.). Knowing and understanding their needs and how they fit into your life will strengthen those relationships.

Think of these things when considering the type of relationship you want, gifts to buy, communication to maintain, and even when setting boundaries where appropriate.

Who	Description of Need

Friends

Your friends should be people who have a positive effect on your life by being a part of it. They are people who are there for different times in your life, and some are life-long friends. Some are friends because of your kids. We want to encourage you to also be open to eliminating those friends who only bring negativity or drama to your life. Sometimes people are only meant to be in your life for a "season," even when there is nothing negative. Appreciate what they mean to you, but be willing to walk away as appropriate.

Below, make a list of your closest friends and list their positive influence in your life.

Name	Impact/Valued Characteristic	Years Known

GOALS

Balance is not the ultimate goal as you design your own life; it's being aware and adjusting if necessary. As you continue through the remaining exercises in this section, remember that you're in charge of your life, and the best way to leverage that control is to be crystal clear on your goals. Documenting a description of your perfect month, noting areas of personal improvement, crafting your Balance Wheel of Life, and Resultsboarding are excellent ways to clarify what you want and how you're going to get there.

> **WHEN YOU DESIGN YOUR OWN LIFE, EVERY DAY AND EVERY MONTH IS A WEEKEND!**

PERFECT MONTH

Imagine that your life is actually a vacation – enjoying day after day of relaxation. Excitement, fun, serenity – when you design your own life, every day and every month is a weekend! The first step is to identify what your ideal month would be like, and then make it happen.

Instructions

What does your perfect month look like? So many components can go into your ideal time-spend, including when you wake up and what you do first every day, what you accomplish and how, what you do NOT get involved in doing, and how you spend your down-time (meditation, self-reflection, time with family, etc.). As you think about your month, include specifics on work, travel, home life, exercise, etc.

Example

Weekday	Rise early; make phone calls/send emails first thing; work with ideal clients on optimal projects; operate with little to no stress; minimize time in traffic; build my business incrementally; spend time with wife/family; exercise for at least 30 minutes; eat nutritionally; "wind down" with self-reflection; get adequate sleep.
Weekend	Enjoy good weather/sunshine; attend a church service; do something fun with kids (festival, game, concert, movies); see friends or extended family; keep up with my exercise routine; do acts of service for my spouse; work on and enjoy my home; go on a date with my spouse; find time for solitude and meditation.
Month	Take 2 – 3 trips maximum for business and 1 trip for pleasure; work on my life plan and Resultsboard (one hour minimum); read at least 3 books and take one continuing education course; volunteer at least 2 hours; add ___% to savings; plan something really special for my family (party, getaway, etc.); make time for parents/grandparents.

My Perfect Month

Weekday	
Weekend	
Month	

Personal Improvement

Everyone can improve, and the most successful are on a path of continual self-reflection, assessment, focus, and refinement. But as with other aspects of designing your own life, you need to clarify and document what you want to change or capitalize on before you can really strategically leverage who and where you are and where you are going.

Balance Wheel of Life

The Balance Wheel is not about having perfect balance; it's that we want to be able to manage balance. For instance, in our early 20s we are often more focused on education, on home life in our 30s, and so on. What we want to encourage is managing balance in six vital areas:

> The Balance Wheel is not about having perfect balance; it's that we want to be able to manage balance.

1. **Spiritual**: Spiritual balance helps guide and gives direction.
2. **Social**: A healthy, fun life that has a social aspect that brings happiness.
3. **Educational**: Continual learning is crucial, be it formal (university) or informal (reading, listening, staying current on world issues).
4. **Home and Family Life**: An atmosphere of faithfulness and commitment will ensure that your family thrives.
5. **Physical/Health**: Your health is extremely important to having a satisfying, productive life. (Refer back to the previous Health Assessment to guide you in this important area.)
6. **Financial**: Financial responsibility translates into many things: peace of mind, the ability to donate to charitable causes, security for children, pleasure, etc.

Instructions

What's your balance wheel of life? Using examples on the next page, and keeping the above area descriptions in mind, document what you want to focus on, as well as the key words that resonate the most with the goal.

Example

Spiritual
Mission Statement: Be Christ-like

Goals	Key Words
1. Be involved and serve in our church	Involved
2. Completely read and study the Bible	Bible
3. Have a great basic understanding of the Bible	Bible
4. Create a visual tool that reminds me of my commitments	Commitment
5. Improve commitments to friends by sharing and giving	Commitment

Social
Mission Statement: Enjoy many relationships

Goals	Key Words
1. Have 10 close couples and family friends	Travel
2. Share dinner, new places, things with our close friends	Dinner
3. Always demonstrate the privilege of giving to my friends know I am a giver, "altruism" from the heart	Give
4. Serve others	Serve
5. Choose friends with similar values and goals	Values

Educational
Mission Statement: Improve my wisdom

Goals	Key Words
1. Be known as wise and worth listening to	Value
2. Read/go through 50-100+ books/CDs per year	Study
3. Enhance and develop a more organized and concise library	Library
4. Know much and keep up with computer knowledge and equipment	Computer
5. Research and write 100 published works	100

Home and Family Life
Mission Statement: Be a model father, husband, and friend

Goals	Key Words
1. Have a loving, comfortable, clean, organized home environment	Home
2. Continue loving, giving, and growing relationship with my wife	Marriage
3. Raise, healthy, happy, and confident children	Family
4. Enjoy and give to my family love and support for their goals	Example
5. Continue to enjoy and improve our home(s) for us	Home

Physical/Health
Mission Statement: Live a life of ultimate health

Goals	Key Words
1. Stretch daily	Stretch
2. Exercise for health (relax) as well as tone	Relax
3. Eat good healthy food prepared in healthy ways	Diet
4. Walk/jog and enjoy physical activity	Exercise
5. Enjoy playing sports that contribute to my health goals	Sports

Financial
Mission Statement: Be debt free, then financially independent

Goals	Key Words
1. Be (personal recourse) debt free	Debt Free
2. Be financially independent for life	Independent
3. Reduce debt to zero and build our trusts	Trusts
4. Constant measurement of critical success factors/scorecard	Measurement
5. Save more than $_____ per year	Save

My Balance Wheel of Life

Spiritual

Mission Statement:

Goals	Key Words
1.	
2.	
3.	
4.	
5.	

Social

Mission Statement:

Goals	Key Words
1.	
2.	
3.	
4.	
5.	

Educational

Mission Statement:

Goals	Key Words
1.	
2.	
3.	
4.	
5.	

Home and Family Life

Mission Statement:

Goals	Key Words
1.	
2.	
3.	
4.	
5.	

Physical/Health

Mission Statement:

Goals	Key Words
1.	
2.	
3.	
4.	
5.	

Financial

Mission Statement:

Goals	Key Words
1.	
2.	
3.	
4.	
5.	

Visionboard (Resultsboard) – Level 2

In Section 1, I introduced the topic of Resultsboarding to create real, tangible results, and encouraged you to start a simple version with very high level vision images.

Instructions

Now is the time to ramp it up by getting even more specific and granular about what you pin to your cork board, which might need to increase in size. You can use some of the key takeaways from the Section 2 exercises you've completed thus far, and add even more images now that you have greater clarity on what you want to do, have, and become.

My Level 2 Resultsboard Ideas

SECTION 2 SUMMARY

You're two thirds of the way through designing your own life! I now encourage you to take a moment to both congratulate yourself and self-reflect again, just as you did in Section 2.

What was the most eye-opening part of your discovery within this section?

Why was that important to you? Why was it significant?

Ready to move from Great to Mastery? Section 3 will help you get even more results with your intentionally planned life.

Section 3 - Mastery (Level 3)

Introduction

The belief that greatness already exists becomes the enemy of mastery. In other words, while thinking great is good enough, there are so many more rewards and results you will see if you're operating in mastery.

Section 2 should have helped you clarify quite a bit of useful information that relates to your life, including where you are, where you want to go, and what you want to become. This section will take you to the next level, and push you to get really specific about who you are personally and professionally.

> **The belief that greatness already exists becomes the enemy of mastery.**

The following exercises will document your talents so that you can better leverage them; help you understand the power of leveraging insight into personality styles (both yours and others'); create a timeline of events that have shaped you and provided you with your current philosophy and perspective; list places you've visited that have influenced you; and craft your personal daily standards, something I personally rely on every day to see success and keep my HLAs aligned with my values, strategy, and vision.

And as a professional, this section will help you hone in on the business experiences that have shaped you; document the milestones that brought you to your current point; describe your ideal client/customer; and document business personal standards that will help you and your team see wins with greater efficiency and less stress.

Additionally, you will clarify your Life Guidelines (what truly makes you who you are); your relationships; and, perhaps most important of all, the goals you have before you that sum up every aspect of your success, including what you find valuable, how you want your home to be, and your "bucket list."

I know that after you complete the exercises in this section, you will be on the path to mastery; and with continual reflection and refinement, you will begin to live the purposeful, intentional, strategic life you personally designed.

Who I am Personally

Your personal philosophy, quite simply, drives what you do and presents who you are. It's comprised of so many aspects and nuances; and even though no one knows you better than yourself, getting clear insight into and then documenting these specifics can be a daunting task. I have found that knowing and leveraging talents is incredibly valuable, as is knowing how to both communicate to others and filter information based on how we as humans are hard-wired from a personality standpoint. Also important is knowing how the past has shaped the present, since this awareness can help you strategically shape the future. Once you have all of this information at your fingertips, you can then develop some personal standards that will guide the days ahead, keeping your values and vision top of mind.

Talents

You are defined not only by who you are, but what you excel at doing and how those talents affect others in your life. Maybe you're a skilled networker or have an affinity for meeting deadlines. Whatever your talents, you can leverage them to help YOU win, and also offer them up to help OTHERS win in ways that are meaningful to them, creating reciprocity down the line.

> YOU ARE DEFINED NOT ONLY BY WHO YOU ARE, BUT WHAT YOU EXCEL AT DOING AND HOW THOSE TALENTS AFFECT OTHERS IN YOUR LIFE.

Instructions

Do you really know your talents and strengths, especially as others see them? Ask people in your life what they see as your top three biggest talents (email is an easy way to do this); you might just be surprised. I've shared the results of a recent request to some of my most trusted advisors below.

Example

Talents	Who Says?
Perseverance; opportunity identification; networking	Jim N.
Connecting quickly with any audience; high energy, focused knowledge and enthusiasm when presenting; credibility	Jim M.
Organization; focus; tenacity	Buz B.
Big thinker; entrepreneurial drive; consistent activity toward goals	Kyle W.
Enthusiasm; persistent (persistence); vision	George L.
Strategist; connector; outside-the-box thinker	Tawnya A.
Perseverance to achieve results; people connector; roadblock buster!	Eloise W.
Leveraging others' talents to exceed expectations; driving for completion; thinking constantly about how to improve	Sara W.

My Top Talents

Talents	Who Says?

PERSONALITY STYLES

There are many different types of assessments used today. We like to use the DISC personality assessment because we believe it gives an accurate, simple explanation of the four specific personality types. Below is a diagram and a brief description of each type.

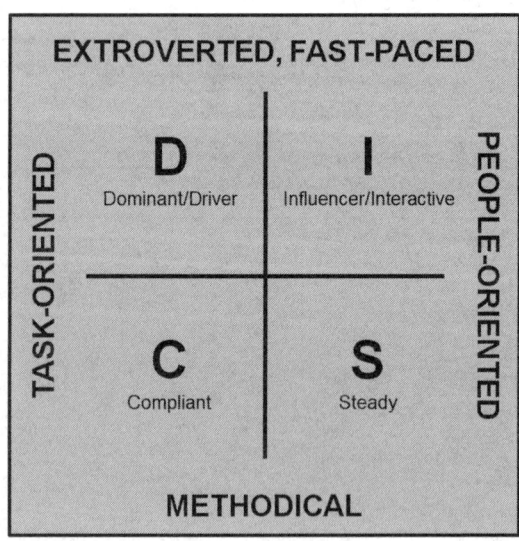

Examples

D = Dominant/Driver

    Key Characteristics:
- Driven by need to be in charge and achieve
- Goal-oriented go-getters
- Focus on no-nonsense approaches to results

    How to Adapt to Driver/Dominant Style
- Don't waste their time (they're time sensitive)
- Be organized and to the point
- Give bottom-line information with options (in writing)
- Appeal to sense of accomplishment—they're goal-oriented

I = Influencer/Interactive

    Key Characteristics:
- Friendly, enthusiastic, like to be with the action
- Thrive on admiration, acknowledgment and compliments
- Persuasive and warm; build great alliances
- Optimistic and charismatic

    How to Adapt to Influencer/Interactive Style
- Give recognition freely
- Support their ideas and opinions
- Be ready to be social with them and get to know them

S = Steady

    Key Characteristics:
- Warm and nurturing (very people-oriented)
- Relaxed disposition makes them approachable
- Loyal
- Risk-averse

    How to Adapt to Steady Style
- Earn their trust and show sincere interest
- Talk feelings, not facts (want approval)
- Never back into a corner

C = Compliant

    Key Characteristics:
- Analytical, persistent, and systematic problem-solvers
- Detail-oriented
- Enjoy perfecting processes and working to results
- High expectations of selves and others (can be critical)

    How to Adapt to Compliant Style
- Be sensitive to their time
- Give them data, details
- Be systematic, logical, well-prepared, and exact

Instructions

We encourage you to find out what your style is. Go to www.tonyjeary.com/bookstore to take the online assessment, then document your style and key takeaways (click on the Other tab and the DISCstyles™ Leadership Report will be accessible). You can also ask that the people in your life do the same, so that you can more effectively communicate with them to create wins all around.

My Personality Style

Personality Style:	
Key Takeaways:	

Others' Personality Styles

Name	
Personality Style:	
Key Takeaways:	

Name	
Personality Style:	
Key Takeaways:	

Name	
Personality Style:	
Key Takeaways:	

Personal Events of Great Meaning

In every life, there are "moments of truth" – happenings of great meaning that possibly impact you for a lifetime. These can be happenings such as a childhood vacation, a milestone birthday party, job promotion, birth of a child; anything that has influenced you. If you will capture and journal these events consistently, you can gain tremendous benefit by encouraging yourself to learn from the past and create a better future.

Instructions

What brought you to where you are today? Today, document just five life events of significance, but continue to think about them. Keep the list growing as you remember more moments that mattered.

Example

As you think about and document your significant life events, consider the following ideas as thought-catalysts:

- First favors and moments of self-awareness
- Lessons, education, mentoring, classes, tutoring
- Hobby accomplishments, sports wins
- Birthdays (yours and others'), anniversaries, deaths
- Vacations as a child and adult
- Influential buildings (grandparents' house, first home you purchased)
- Material possessions you worked hard to attain (cars, homes, etc.)
- Mistakes or learning lessons
- Memorable gifts (to you and from you)
- Spiritual awakenings
- Financial milestones
- Business successes/promotions
- Dates of note (meeting your spouse, birth of child or children, wedding)
- Interesting accomplishments (walking on fire, skydiving, scuba diving)
- Involvement in groups, clubs, associations
- Meeting mentors, advisors, coaches, friends

- Transitions (yours and others', including spouse, children, grandchildren)

My Significant Life Events

Event	Date	Takeaway
1.		
2.		
3.		
4.		
5.		
6.		
7.		
8.		
9.		
10.		
11.		
12.		
13.		
14.		
15.		
16.		
17.		
18.		
19.		
20.		

PLACES OF INFLUENCE

Over the course of a lifetime, we are exposed to people and places that play a role in shaping our lives. Many of these can be linked to our involvement in various "institutions" such as churches and schools.

Instructions

Who helped you become YOU? Know yourself better and identify more of "why" you do what you do by listing out the institutions that impacted you, and how you changed as a result.

Example

Think through the following categories as you document your places of influence:

- Preschool
- Grade school
- Middle school
- High school
- College/university
- Churches
- Personal clubs
- Professional organizations

My Places of Influence

Influencing Institution	Impact
1.	
2.	
3.	
4.	
5.	
6.	
7.	
8.	
9.	
10.	

Personal Daily Standards

Your Personal Daily Standards are those standards that you strive to live by and operate from. This can include a spiritual side, some of your prior business standards, and any other items that are important to you that help you run a happy and healthy life.

Instructions

How do you personally conduct yourself every day? Below, I have shared the guiding principles that I rely on every day to make the most of the life in front of me, and to see the results I want. Document your own, then print out and post wherever you can reflect on them often.

Example

Tony's Personal Daily Standards
• Ask in prayer for smartness and Holy Spirit support and alignment with God's will
• Do team huddles often to keep priorities aligned and communication clear
• Glance at "pipe" each morning to have actions fresh in mind
• Determine VIPs for the day using a master list
• Touch team members inspirationally
• Communicate appreciation to all those around me (personal and professional)
• Organize (rationalize) so more good things can come in
• Visualize with further "clarity" goals, direction, vision, and refinement
• Model exceptional behavior including enjoying life
• Eat healthy
• Do favors and help advance my clients' success

My Personal Daily Standards

Personal Daily Standards

Who I am Professionally

Business Experiences

We are, in part, defined by our professional experiences, whether we've worked for others, owned/founded our own company, or advised/consulted for a third party. We obviously learn from the mistakes and successes encountered during our jobs/experiences, and maybe even more so from our colleagues, mentors, supervisors, or clients. Anyone we encounter professionally can have an impact.

Instructions

What professional experiences mattered most? Take a look back and think about how you've spent your professional life, and document your history – oftentimes this can trigger ideas, best practices, and inspiration to bring more value to your world today.

Example

Much like your resume, you will want to think through where you have worked and when, and in what capacity – but an important distinction here is to document the key takeaways, or lessons, from that experience (positive or negative, since everything can be a learning experience). Some examples of key takeaways might include:

- Learning business principles/lessons
- Exceeding expectations
- Working with a negative manager/colleague
- Being promoted on merit
- Increasing responsibility through hard work
- Helping someone win
- Managing a team
- Mentoring others to increase their skill set
- Overcoming an obstacle, roadblock, or challenge
- Realizing something valuable about yourself
- Receiving accolades or awards
- Experiencing moments of personal growth
- Developing processes or procedures of note

- Producing/publishing a tool of great use
- Taking on ever-growing responsibility
- Dealing with hurdles, criticism, praise, apathy
- Training others on best practices
- Feeling very accomplished for specific reasons

My Professional History

Year	Company/Employer	Title/Role	Key Takeaways

Ideal Professional Situation

As a professional, it's important to know when you provide the most value and thrive (benefiting both yourself and others). Beyond being aware of and leveraging your talents, insight into personality styles, and lessons learned throughout your career, you need to know the ideal client, customer, project type, etc. that capitalizes on everything you bring to the table. This knowledge will also help you avoid situations in which you will not be able to operate at peak, and instead you can choose other opportunities for greater wins and less stress.

> **AS A PROFESSIONAL, IT'S IMPORTANT TO KNOW WHEN YOU PROVIDE THE MOST VALUE AND THRIVE.**

Instructions

When and for whom do you perform the best? Identify your ideal situation by type as well as the characteristics of each.

Example

Think through actual and desired people, companies, individuals, projects, situations, etc. and what the ideal characteristics are for each. Ideal characteristics can include things like timely/quick payment, having a certain level of success, working with a certain role within a company, fulfilling a need, having a flexible deadline, being particularly challenging/enjoyable, etc.

My Ideal Professional Situation

Type	Characteristics

PROFESSIONAL DAILY STANDARDS

Business standards represent how you run your professional life and can range from being on time, organized, prepared, etc. How well you (and your time) execute these standards will have a direct impact on how the world perceives you as a business person.

Instructions

How do you conduct yourself professionally every day? This is so important that I am going to share, in the example below, you my personal business standards to get your thoughts going. Spend some time developing and documenting your own personal business standards, using my example as a springboard.

Example

Tony's Professional Daily Standards
• *Save Tony's time, keeping him in front of and serving our clients* • *Kaizen means constant improvement for all team members...on-going COEs, personal SWOTs and MOLO refinements* • *Keep all clean and organized...adds to our brand and makes us always ready* • *Constant list making...ensures prioritizing, accountability, and execution of faster results (including CSFs)* • *Over-communicate and calculate...helps ensure efforts are maximized* • *Avoid absolutes - words like "never, always, can't"* • *Focus efforts on new flow of business/revenue* • *Do (FIA) favors in advance - sharing, giving, and helping others win* • *Do things now - operate with a mindset of quick action and speed to completion while using "production before perfection" - manage procrastination* • *Proactive everything (think ahead, prep ahead, do ahead, invoice ahead, deliver ahead and exceed expectations all around - internally and externally)* • *Team approach - overlap, cross-support, encourage, leverage each other's expertise, and together keep all eyes on getting things done and completed and results produced*

My Professional Daily Standards

Professional Daily Standards

LIFE GUIDELINES

We all want results and success, but who we are as people is more than just a checklist of things to accomplish. It's important to focus on our hearts, not only our heads, and counting our blessings is a great way to start. Also useful is thinking about and documenting the influence others have had on shaping our lives, either through books/quotes (as discussed in Section 2) or best practices.

Thankfulness/Gratitude

Kurt Vonnegut once said, "Remember the little things in life… one day you will find out that they were the big things." It is so easy in life to get caught up in the attainment of "big things" and not realize that it is the "little things" in our lives that often bring us the greatest joy.

> REMEMBER THE LITTLE THINGS IN LIFE… ONE DAY YOU WILL FIND OUT THAT THEY WERE THE BIG THINGS.

Instructions

What should you appreciate, and why? One of the most powerful tools for defeating discouragement is the principle of "counting your blessings." Below, list the best things about your life, and why they matter.

Example

Things such as health, speech, sight, family, freedom, intellect, friends, etc., give life meaning and ultimately purpose. Each and every day is a gift. That's not to say that we shouldn't be thankful for material things as well. Having a roof over our head, food, clothing, a career, should be cause to give thanks as well. Think through everything positive in your life.

My Top 10 Blessings

Blessing	Details
1.	
2.	
3.	
4.	
5.	
6.	
7.	
8.	
9.	
10.	

FAVORITE BOOKS OF IMPACT

Favorite books that are impacting the way you live your life are great to have at your fingertips to continue to feed learning and guidelines for moving forward and always striving to be better.

Instructions

What books have had the most impact? List the book, and include the key takeaway or core concept of the book to show why it had impact for you. Go back and list books you've read years ago as well as new ones. Add to the list continually. And, if you discover you have not read as much as you would have liked, consider listing some books you would like to read in the future.

Example

I have compiled a list of 100 books that have had an impact on my life:
1. *The Art of War,* Sun Tzu
2. *The Art of Worldly Wisdom,* Blatasar Gracian
3. *The Way to Wealth,* Benjamin Franklin
4. *Message to Garcia,* Elbert Hubbard

5. *As a Man Thinketh*, James Allen
6. *The Science of Getting Rich*, Wallace Wattles
7. *How We Think*, John Dewey
8. *The Autobiography of Andrew Carnegie*, Andrew Carnegie
9. *Acres of Diamonds*, Russell H. Conwell
10. *My Life and Work*, Henry Ford
11. *The Richest Man in Babylon*, George S. Clason
12. *The Law of Success*, Napoleon Hill
13. *How to Win Friends and Influence People*, Dale Carnegie
14. *Think and Grow Rich*, Napoleon Hill
15. *The Magic of Believing*, Claude M Bristol
16. *The Power of Positive Thinking*, Norman Vincent Peale
17. *Motivation and Personality*, Abraham Maslow
18. *The Practice of Management*, Peter F. Drucker
19. *The Strangest Secret*, Earl Nightingale
20. *How to Have Confidence and Power in Dealing with People*, Les Giblin
21. *The Magic of Thinking Big*, David J. Schwartz
22. *Man's Search for Meaning*, Viktor E. Frankl
23. *Success through a Positive Mental Attitude*, Napoleon Hill and W. Clement Stone
24. *Psycho-Cybernetics*, Maxwell Maltz
25. *The Greatest Salesman in the World*, Og Mandino
26. *See You at the Top*, Zig Ziglar
27. *Gifts Differing: Understanding Personality Type*, Isabel Briggs Myers
28. *The Seasons of Life*, Jim Rohn and Ronald Reynolds
29. *The One-Minute Manager*, Kenneth H. Blanchard and Spencer Johnson
30. *In Search of Excellence: Lessons from America's Best-Run Companies*, Thomas J. Peters and Robert H. Waterman Jr.
31. *The Official Guide to Success*, Tom Hopkins
32. *Unlimited Power*, Anthony Robbins
33. *Influence: The Psychology of Persuasion*, Robert B. Cialdini
34. *The Psychology of Winning*, Denis Waitley
35. *The E-Myth* (the original), Michael E. Gerber
36. *The 7 Habits of Highly Effective People*, Stephen R. Covey

37. *Moments of Truth*, Jan Carlzon
38. *Swim with the Sharks Without Being Eaten Alive*, Harvey MacKay
39. *Flow: The Psychology of Optimal Experience*, Mihaly Csikszentmihalyi
40. *Learned Optimism*, Martin Seligman
41. *Five Major Pieces to the Life Puzzle*, Jim Rohn
42. *Lincoln on Leadership*, Donald T Phillips
43. *Made in America*, Sam Walton
44. *Paradigms: The Business of Discovering the Future*, Joel A. Barker
45. *Maximum Achievement*, Brian Tracy
46. *Chicken Soup for the Soul Series*, Jack Canfield and Mark Victor Hansen
47. *Emotional Intelligence*, Daniel Goleman
48. *The Aladdin Factor*, Jack Canfield and Mark Victor Hansen
49. *The Spellbinders Gift*, Og Mandino
50. *Creativity: Flow, and the Psychology of Discovery and Invention*, Mihaly Csikszentmihalyi
51. *The Millionaire Next Door: The Surprising Secrets of America's Wealthy*, Thomas J. Stanley and William D. Danko
52. *How to Argue and Win Every Time: At Home, At Work, In Court, Everywhere, Every Day*, Gerry Spence
53. *The Spirit to Serve*, J.W. Marriott Jr.
54. *The 48 Laws of Power*, Robert Greene
55. *The Platinum Rule*, Tony Alessandra
56. *Cashflow Quadrant: Rich Dad's Guide to Financial Freedom*, Robert Kiyosaki
57. *The Acorn Principle*, Jim Cathcart
58. *Selling to VITO: The Very Important Top Officer*, Anthony Parinello
59. *Charisma – Seven Keys to Developing the Magnetism That Leads to Success*, Dr. Tony Alessandra
60. *Rich Dad, Poor Dad*, Robert T. Kiyosaki
61. *The Tipping Point: How Little Things Can Make a Big Difference*, Malcolm Gladwell
62. *The Millionaire Mind*, Thomas J Stanley
63. *The Power of Focus*, Jack Canfield, Mark Victor Hansen, Les Hewitt
64. *Now, Discover Your Strengths*, Marcus Buckingham

65. *Getting Things Done: The Art of Stress-Free Productivity,* David Allen
66. *The Five Dysfunctions of a Team: A Leadership Fable,* Patrick Lencioni
67. *Value Based Fees: How to Charge – and – Get What You're Worth,* Alan Weiss
68. *The One-Minute Millionaire: The Enlightened Way to Wealth,* Mark Victor Hansen and Robert G. Allen
69. *Purple Cow,* Seth Godin
70. *Law of Attraction,* Michael Losier
71. *Managing By Values: How to Put Your Values into Action for Extraordinary Results,* Ken Blanchard and Michael O'Connor
72. *The Art of Exceptional Living,* Jim Rohn
73. *Life Is a Series of Presentations,* Tony Jeary, Kim Dower, and J.E. Fishman
74. *Live a Thousand Years: Have The Time of Your Life,* Giovanni Livera
75. *The Art of the Start: The Time-Tested, Battle-Hardened Guide for Anyone Starting Anything,* Guy Kawasaki
76. *High Visibility: Transforming Your Personal and Professional Brand,* Irving Rein, Philip Kotler, Michael Hamlin, and Martin Stoller
77. *Blue Ocean Strategy: How to Create Uncontested Market Space and Make Competition Irrelevant,* W. Chan Kim and Renée Mauborgne
78. *Blink: The Power of Thinking Without Thinking,* Malcolm Gladwell
79. *Keys to the Vault: Lessons From the Pros on Raising Money and Igniting Your Business,* Keith Cunningham
80. *The Number: A Completely Different Way to Think about the Rest of Your Life,* Lee Eisenberg
81. *The Richest Man Who Ever Lived,* Steven S. Scott
82. *The Speed of Trust: The One Thing That Changes Everything,* Stephen M.R. Covey
83. *24 Keys That Bring Complete Success,* Paul Meyer
84. *How to Get Anything You Want,* Nido Qubein
85. *The 4-Hour Workweek,* Tim Ferris
86. *The Psychology of Selling,* Brian Tracy
87. *The Black Swan,* Nassim Nicholas Taleb
88. *Life Entrepreneurs,* Christopher Gergen
89. *Outliers: The Story of Success,* Malcolm Gladwell

90. *Tribes,* Seth Godin
91. *Strategic Acceleration,* Tony Jeary
92. *Be Great: The Five Foundations of an Extraordinary Life in Business—and Beyond,* Peter Thomas
93. *Flourish,* Martin Seligman
94. *Thinking, Fast and Slow,* Daniel Kahneman
95. *Born to Win,* Zig Ziglar
96. *Drive: The Surprising Truth about What Moves Us,* Daniel H. Pink
97. *The Power of Habit: Why We Do What We Do,* Charles Duhigg
98. *you2: A High-Velocity Formula for Multiplying Your Personal Effectiveness in Quantum Leaps,* Price Pritchett
99. *The One Thing: The Surprisingly Simple Truth Behind Extraordinary Results,* Gary Keller
100. *Business Ground Rules,* Tony Jeary, Peter Thomas, and Tammy Kling

My Favorite Books of Impact

Title	Takeaway
1.	
2.	
3.	
4.	
5.	
6.	
7.	
8.	
9.	
10.	
11.	
12.	
13.	
14.	
15.	
16.	
17.	
18.	
19.	
20.	

Relationships

Raving Fans

In his book *Raving Fans*, Ken Blanchard describes the goal of outstanding customer service or client satisfaction. The idea is not to create more happy customers – it's to create raving fans, people who will hire you as a client, refer you to others, and in general support you in any way within their means. And they genuinely like you.

Instructions

Who are the raving fans in your life? Keep their names and contact information within reach to use as needed, and be ready to reciprocate for them as well.

My Raving Fans

Name	Role/Value	Phone	Email

People of Most Influence (POI)

I hope you've been as fortunate as I have to experience, learn from, and even coach some truly unique, influential individuals. They have helped me win so many times, and in so many ways; I am so blessed to have them on my life team. I think of them often, and frequently consider ways I can give back, help them, or brighten their day.

Instructions

Who has helped shape your life? List the persons, their role to you, and how you can bring value to their world.

Example

There are so many other people who have shaped my life and career that listing them all here would be cumbersome for you to read; but think of all of your gifts and who brought them to you as you complete your own list. The individuals who have influenced me most include my father, who was a fantastic model from whom I learned to serve, share, network, and make lists. My father-in-law, a generous and kind man, has helped guide how I father my two beautiful, brilliant daughters over the years. My former president, the late and great Jim Norman, helped me reshape how I think, and transformed my business priorities. Zig Ziglar had a tremendous impact on me as I was just starting out; he taught me about setting goals and being successful, while remaining a humble Christian. Robert Schuller and Tony Robbins both taught me the power of thinking of possibilities and taking risks, and Tom Peters showed me how to maximize my brand.

My People of Most Influence (POI)

Name	Role	My Value to Them

ADVISORS

"A wise person learns from both the mistakes and successes of others." In my book *Advice Matters* I write at length about how seeking advice from others who have achieved the kind of results you're looking for is one of the wisest – and quickest – ways to design and live a successful life, grow your business, and/or hit that next level of success you've been endeavoring to reach.

The most successful people understand that they need to surround themselves with individuals who can pour into them the wisdom and knowledge they need to excel. When people think of seeking advice to help them make wise decisions and improve their results, they generally think of mentors and/or coaches. While both help you uncover *Blind Spots* and can exponentially advance your life and career to the next level,

> **SEEKING ADVICE FROM OTHERS WHO HAVE ACHIEVED THE KIND OF RESULTS YOU'RE LOOKING FOR IS ONE OF THE WISEST – AND QUICKEST – WAYS TO DESIGN AND LIVE A SUCCESSFUL LIFE.**

there is a difference. Coaches are paid for their advice, while mentors offer free advice. Each has its own distinctive advantage. The best scenario is to seek out the advice of at least one coach who will challenge and inspire you to be your best and one or more mentors who will give you the benefit of their wisdom, experience, and insight.

Then, as you go through life, you often find people you relate to and admire, and you may bounce things off of each other. Those people are not really a coach or a mentor; they are colleagues that you trust and look up to for advice. And sometimes you will hire people – like attorneys, CPAs, or financial planners – to bring you expertise in certain areas. They're not really a coach or a mentor either; they're paid advisors.

Instructions

Who influences your world? Capture below the advisors in your life – you probably have some you haven't even thought about. I also encourage you to think about areas where you could add some as well that can help you accomplish your goals. List your advisors below.

Example

As you think about the six sources of advice in your life – mentors, coaches, trusted colleagues, advisors, resources, and yourself – consider that many of the really successful people in life are open-minded and use a solid mix of all six to help them live in the level of Mastery.

My Advisors

Name	Role	Impact/Valued Characteristics
1.		
2.		
3.		
4.		
5.		
6.		
7.		
8.		
9.		
10.		
11.		
12.		
13.		
14.		
15.		

MY LIFE TEAM

This is a master list of people helping you make things happen. Top Performers have big teams – I have over 50 on mine!

Instructions

Who helps you "do life?" List the most obvious members of your Life Team below, including their role and why you've chosen them to help you.

Example

Life Team members can include contractors, medical support, attorneys, counselors, employees, household help, professional service providers (plumber, CPA, horticulturist), personal assistants, researchers, spiritual advisors, insurance professionals, financial advisors, hair/clothing stylists… the list is endless.

My Life Team

Name	Role	Impact/Valued Characteristics
1.		
2.		
3.		
4.		
5.		
6.		
7.		
8.		
9.		
10.		
11.		
12.		
13.		
14.		
15.		

Intentional Congruence

Intentional Congruence is about being "intentional" in understanding how people fit into your life and gathering those people in such a way that you can stay focused on your own HLAs more consistently.

Instructions

How does your entire life fit together? Create a list of people who are influential to you in various ways, personally and professionally. Next, attempt to create a mind map that depicts this sphere of influence. Include your immediate family, your church, your schools, your advisors (CPA, insurance, etc.), people who help you run your home, your company(ies), key people within your company, etc.

Example

Use the below example as a guide.

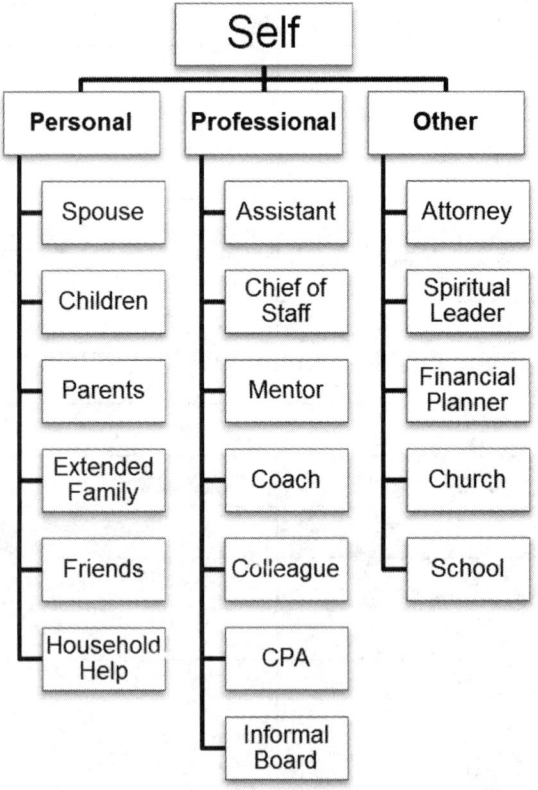

My Intentional Congruence Map

GOALS

10 Times as Valuable

There are daily HLAs that matter most for short-term results, but there are also longer-term areas of focus that could potentially make you 10 times as valuable if you were to commit to concentrating on them.

Instructions

How could your life be 10 times better? Take some time and begin listing people and actions that will really make a difference in your personal and professional effectiveness. It could be things you already know to do, but just haven't set goals to do them. Continue to add things on an ongoing basis.

Example

Ask yourself, *How Can I:*
- Strengthen my relationship with my spouse?
- Become debt free?
- Maximize my advisors?
- Be more effective?
- Be more disciplined, determined, confident, persistent, and focused?
- Improve my relationship with God?
- Strengthen family relationships?
- Live a life of ultimate health?
- Have greater financial strength?
- Maximize my contacts/network/Life Team?
- Educate and improve my wisdom?
- Perfect my business strengths?
- Delegate better?
- Remain organized?
- Enjoy every day?
- Maximize technology?
- Increase negotiating strength?
- Maximize my brand?

My "10 Times as Valuable" Matrix

What	Potential Impact
1.	
2.	
3.	
4.	
5.	
6.	
7.	
8.	
9.	
10.	
11.	
12.	
13.	
14.	
15.	

Likeness

Modeling and learning from others who have lives we admire or successes we also seek is a great way to get results. Just as advice matters, so does identifying and implementing distinctions from individuals who are maybe just a little further down the same path you're on.

Instructions

Who can I model, and why? Below, list who and what you want to model, why, and how.

> **Modeling and learning from others who have lives we admire or successes we also seek is a great way to get results.**

Example

Things on the Likeness Matrix should be those companies, organizations or people you see that you want to mirror or be like. Note the specifics you'd like to duplicate so you have true clarity in your mind. Some of my examples are below:

Example Likeness Matrix

Model	Distinction	How
1. Joel Katz - Office Team Support	Valet service, details handled	Staff
2. Ritz Carlton - Environment	Pristine, organized, clean	Juan and staff
3. Cesar's Palace - Grounds	Manicured, flawless	Gardeners, lawn service
4. Japanese Hotel Garden - Picnic Area	Serene, peaceful	Gardeners, lawn service
5. Kyle Wilson - Database	Large, organized, systematic	Software and dedication
6. Brian Tracy - Affiliate/Promoter Databank	Large, organized, systematic	Software and nourishment
7. Zig Ziglar - Reputation	Esteemed, respected, Christian	Follow-through
8. Jerry Johnson - Accounting	Daily critical success factors	Clarity and systems
9. Ken Blanchard - Brand	Business guru	Breakthrough book
10. Dale Carnegie - Business Legacy	Life, presentations, evergreen	Continued focus

My Likeness Matrix

Model	Distinction	How
1.		
2.		
3.		
4.		
5.		
6.		
7.		
8.		
9.		
10.		
11.		
12.		
13.		
14.		
15.		

Home Improvement

Many people enjoy building and improving their home(s). Being clearer on and actually documenting what you'd like to add, improve, or remodel can be inspiring and draw you toward that accomplishment.

Instructions

How can your home be better? Make a list of home improvements you'd like to do over the next one to five years. These can be inside or outside and might include an estimated budget.

My Home Improvement Matrix

What	Value-Add	Cost
1.		
2.		
3.		
4.		
5.		
6.		
7.		
8.		
9.		
10.		
11.		
12.		
13.		
14.		
15.		

Timeline of My Projected Life

There is tremendous power in writing things down. I really believe that documenting the things I have wanted to accomplish, do, or see has had a direct impact on my success over the years. On my personal Projected Life list, I am blessed to have been able to cross out several, and I look forward to continuing to execute the many awesome things I envision for my future.

Instructions

What do you want for tomorrow? In the following table, fill in the major events (perhaps in five year increments) that will happen, or that you want to happen over the course of your remaining life. Include the year and age you will be at the time of the goal as part of your timeline.

Example

Ideas include: promotions you anticipate or want, kids going off to college or getting married, having a child, becoming debt free, reaching a certain financial goal, celebrating specific birthday or anniversary milestones, etc. Think of these more as *milestones* than tasks, which will be addressed on your Bucket List later in this section.

My Projected Life Timeline

Goal	Year	Age
1.		
2.		
3.		
4.		
5.		
6.		
7.		
8.		
9.		
10.		

Travel

Seeing the world can provide life-changing experiences, whether it be simple towns or glamorous and exotic places. This is an exercise about appreciating the places you've been and capturing the places you want to go and why.

Instructions

Where do you want to visit? Below, list the countries, cities, and places you've either visited or want to experience.

My Travel Matrix

Countries I've Visited	
Countries I Want to Experience	
Cities I've Visited	
Cities I Want to Experience	

DESIGNING YOUR OWN LIFE

Places I've Visited

Places I Want to Experience

Top 100 Life Goals – Bucket List

By this point in the process, you should have excellent insight into everything you want to accomplish, do, see, own, and become – big and small, right now or later down the line, realistic or fantastic. I love the idea of a Bucket List as it allows for some fun planning without a lot of strategy; it's just a list of stuff you want to do before you die. I have lots of crazy items on my personal bucket list, as well as "normal" ones I am sure I share with a lot of you. The point here is to dream big, and (eventually) have a list of 100 goals that give you pleasure to think about, occasionally rework, and (I hope!) eventually accomplish.

> I LOVE THE IDEA OF A BUCKET LIST AS IT ALLOWS FOR SOME FUN PLANNING WITHOUT A LOT OF STRATEGY; IT'S JUST A LIST OF STUFF YOU WANT TO DO BEFORE YOU DIE.

Instructions

Below, begin listing your top 100 life goals. These are in no particular order or time frame. Just brainstorm and let the goals flow. Don't worry about listing 100 goals right now. The important part is continuing to define and set goals. Put an "x" in the right column when you complete items on the list as the months and years move on.

Example

This could be what some call a "Bucket List" and includes large things, small things, personal and business. Many of them should be "stretch" goals.

My Top 100 Life Goals

Goal	Complete?
1.	
2.	
3.	
4.	
5.	
6.	
7.	
8.	
9.	
10.	
11.	
12.	
13.	
14.	
15.	
16.	
17.	
18.	
19.	
20.	
21.	
22.	
23.	
24.	
25.	
26.	

27.	
28.	
29.	
30.	
31.	
32.	
33.	
34.	
35.	
36.	
37.	
38.	
39.	
40.	
41.	
42.	
43.	
44.	
45.	
46.	
47.	
48.	
49.	
50.	
51.	
52.	
53.	

54.	
55.	
56.	
57.	
58.	
59.	
60.	
61.	
62.	
63.	
64.	
65.	
66.	
67.	
68.	
69.	
70.	
71.	
72.	
73.	
74.	
75.	
76.	
77.	
78.	
79.	
80.	

81.	
82.	
83.	
84.	
85.	
86.	
87.	
88.	
89.	
90.	
91.	
92.	
93.	
94.	
95.	
96.	
97.	
98.	
99.	
100.	

DESIGNING YOUR OWN LIFE

VISIONBOARD (RESULTSBOARD) – LEVEL 3

In Sections 1 and 2, we introduced ever-increasing levels of Resultsboarding, which I have seen really work in my life, as well as the lives of my family, friends, and clients. By now, you have probably completed many of the exercises within this book, and have a clear picture on what you want to have, see, and become, maybe in an "in progress" Resultsboard format.

Instructions

What results are in your vision? If you haven't already started your own Resultsboard, I encourage you to read through the previous instructions and get started, and then move to the Mastery level when you are ready.

Example

Below is an example of my Resultsboard (at Mastery level, which spans the entire length of my gym area. Use this as an example of how to build your own (buying simple corkboard and putting it on a wall can be a good start). In the space below the example, write down items you would want to place on your Resultsboard that you can look up and print (or cut from a magazine). Include your family as well.

My Level 3 Resultsboard Ideas

Section 3 Summary

Congratulations, you've designed your own life in the Mastery level! You are ready to start living out the practices you've identified as most important to your success.

What was the most eye-opening part of your discovery within this section?

Why was that important to you? Why was it significant?

I encourage you to revisit all of these exercises often to keep your outlook fresh and your vision crisp.

Conclusion

The one thing we can agree on, that we all have in common, is that we all want to live a happy, successful, and fulfilling life. Achieving that can sometimes be elusive, but it doesn't have to be. There are too many people who live a life – at least in some ways – other than the one they want, and it is primarily because they haven't *designed* the one they want.

Ask yourself: **is the life you are living right now by accident or on purpose?** It should be more on purpose, and this book is the tool to help you move into purposeful Mastery. You now have the means, processes, best practices, and clarity to create the life you seek – through setting and documenting your goals.

As I've said over and over, I really believe there's a tremendous pulling power to goals. The sheer intentionality of crafting goals gives clarity to your vision and is a driving force for being the most successful you can be. The definition of what makes a person successful is different for each one of us, but there is one factor that is common to all: success rarely happens by accident.

> THE SHEER INTENTIONALITY OF CRAFTING GOALS GIVES CLARITY TO YOUR VISION AND IS A DRIVING FORCE FOR BEING THE MOST SUCCESSFUL YOU CAN BE.

By now you should have greater insight into the power of purposely setting goals; maybe you've even already seen a positive change or a move toward different and better results just from your initial work in this book. You could be consciously seeking out, with purpose, the goals you've identified, and you can bet that your Reticular Activating System is hard at work sorting information in your goals' favor.

You now have a written record of who you are, how you got there, and where you want to go. You have insight into how you excel, what others think of you, and how you can be a better individual, both personally and professionally. I am really hoping you have started a Resultsboard, because

I am living proof that the process works… and I've seen others have similar success with that tool.

Whether you completed one, all, a handful, or the majority of the exercises in this book, I want to congratulate you. You've taken the first step to designing, with strategy and clarity, the life you really want.

Appendices

Table of Contents Cross Reference Matrix

#	Page #	ITEM	WHAT IT IS	THE PURPOSE	HOW TO USE	PRIORITY L / M / H	ACTION BY
				INTRODUCTION			
	5	Why this book	Challenge others to live life more intentionally	Share the purpose of the book and get into right mindset	Read		
	6	Set up	Provide validation for the impact gained from goal-setting	Share concepts of book and get people thinking; share why people don't set goals and explain Belief Window	Read		
	11	My Story	Inspiration for committing to the DYOL process	Give Tony's story with Jim Norman as background to engage the reader and set them up for the journey	Read		
	14	How to Use This Book	Lists the three main sections of the book (Good, Great, Mastery), and sets mind frame for beginning	Helps you plan to get more of what you want	Read		
	16	Conclusion	Leads into the main book sections	Closes the setup for the book	Read		
				SECTION 1: GOOD (LEVEL 1)			
	25	Assess Yourself: Six Goals Areas	Six areas: financial, physical/health, home and family life, educational, social, and spiritual	Describe the six areas and assess self in each area	Assess on 1-10 scale where their starting point is with each		
	26	Values Tournament	60 Values	Identify what matters most to you	Choose your top 10 Values		
	27	High Level Activities (HLAs)	Items that when focused on provide the highest amount of impact	Increase results by focusing on the most impactful things	Write down your top HLAs, for personal and professional		
				Strategic Acceleration Framework			
	29	Personal Framework	A separate snapshot picture for your personal life – purpose, passion/happiness, values, goals, filters, roles, HLAs	Gain focus at-a-glance of what is important to you	Complete the framework document		
	32	Business Framework	A separate and distinct snapshot picture for your business of its objectives, strategies, actions and values	Give professional and/or business clarity of vision with a blueprint to achieve that vision, resulting in realistic and inspirational business processes and plans	First determine whether this will be for your Professional Career or for a Business entity. Understand this specific career or business by documenting its vision & mission which will lead to discovery of the remaining categories		
	35	Vision/Results Board (Level 1)	A tool to facilitate the creation of your vision board - a visual representation of goals in your life	A vision board provides inspiration and motivation every time you look at it	Reflect and list, then collect pictures and items that represent things you are striving for – Use Tony's example as a guide (page 82)		

#	Page #	ITEM	WHAT IT IS	THE PURPOSE	HOW TO USE	PRIORITY L/M/H	ACTION BY
SECTION 2: GREAT (LEVEL 2)							
Who I Am Personally – gain clarity on the various elements that make up who you are and want to be							
	41	Core Beliefs	A tool to discover, document, and analyze your personal belief system	Get clarity & specify the beliefs you filter life by, discover any inaccurate beliefs that negatively affect your thinking, and discover what beliefs you can use & leverage	Answer the self-discovery questions by determining and documenting your beliefs and blind spots		
	44	My Spirituality	A process to discover, document, and analyze the guidelines you use to make decisions and think	Allows you to specify & examine how you are maturing spiritually, and determine weak vs strong areas, and their importance	List your areas of evaluation, rate yourself, then create a list of positive actions in order to improve		
	46	Pains and Pleasures	A tool to enable discovery of the pains to avoid and the pleasures to pursue and experience	Enables you to discover how to enjoy life's journey with less pain and more pleasure	Identify and list specific pains and pleasures to avoid or pursue every day		
	47	Health	A process listing, discovering and documenting specific areas of current health and how to improve	Provides direction and opportunity to live a life of Ultimate Health, as a strong mind and body directly affect your ability to execute your goals	For each specific area of your health, identify what you are doing now and what you want to do in the future		
	50	Accomplishments (and values)	A process to note works and acts you have completed that and are valued by yourself and/or others	Quickly and easily define your accomplishments to discover your values & strengths, appreciate your blessings, and bring clarity to future goals	Create a list of things you have, have shared, experienced, given or become		
Who I Am Professionally – gain clarity on the past, present and future elements that make up who you are, and want to be, professionally							
	53	Your Brand (Personal Branding Matrix)	A tool to discover and document various elements that make up the way others see you	Ensures the various elements of your brand are in sync and congruent with who you are	Review the various elements and record the details to become aware of and ensure your branding supports the way you want others to view you		
	55	Professional Priorities (Desired Work Environment)	An aid to obtaining clarity on the type of elements & environment that you enjoy working in and that best sets you up to operate at maximum effectiveness	Identify what suits you best to maximize your talents and personal style, in order that you are aware of your optimal working environment	Examine and list your preferred work environment qualities and specifics		
	57	Career Interests	A process to list your career interests that you enjoy, in which you believe you could thrive and have success	To identify and become aware of areas of interest that paint a picture of your ideal situation	Reflect and think about, then list, career areas and avenues that interest and inspire you		
	58	Business Strengths	A process to list your current and desired skills, that are or will be an asset to your career	Allows you to become aware of your current strengths & skills, and of ones you want to acquire to further your success	Reflect and list your current strengths & skills, and ones you want to acquire, including the way you think		
	59	Leadership Effectiveness	Twenty five best practices to become a more effective leader	Raises awareness of your strengths and opportunities in the area of leadership	Assess your leadership strengths in twenty five areas under five categories		

#	Page #	ITEM	WHAT IT IS	THE PURPOSE	HOW TO USE	PRIORITY L/M/H	ACTION BY
				Life Guidelines			
	62	MOLO (More Of Less Of)	A process to identify, differentiate and list components of your life (i.e., work, tasks, habits, actions, etc.) into various categories	To make you aware of your high leverage activities, so you can focus on them to get more of what you want out of life	Reflect and identify things you need to do more of, less of, start doing, stop doing and do differently. Fill in the various categories and really think about how changing specific things can change your outcomes		
	65	Habits to Continue or Eliminate	A process to discover, review, analyze then categorize your habits, both good and bad, as they pertain to the various roles you play in life	To provide a mechanism to determine if your current habits are producing all the results you really want	Discover & list the various roles you play in life. Then discover and list your habits in each role, then reflect, analyze, and decide, for each of these habits whether they should be either maintained or eliminated. Finally rate yourself on how well you are playing each role		
	67	Spiritual Life	A tool to identify, document, and thereby gain clarity on the spiritual wisdom that is the foundation to your life	Having and knowing your spiritual guidelines will help you weather life's storms and enable you to better impact the lives of others	Thoughtfully consider then list the spiritual guidelines that are important to you and have impacted your life		
	68	Wisdom to Live By	A tool to document the verses or spiritual sayings that impact your life	Useful in times of need and as a guide for your spiritual life	Take time to draw on your faith and identify quotes or scriptures to live by to help guide you in your spiritual life (page 46)		
	71	Sayings & Quotes	A tool to discover and document quotes and sayings that motivate and inspire you	Provides inspiration and motivation	Allows reflection and focus on things of importance and inspiration		
		Relationships – it is extremely important to understand how relationships and our interactions affect us in the world					
	73	Family Mission Statement & Commitment	A process to open communication then discover and document a family mission statement and desired commitments between and to one another	Promotes family unity, cohesive direction, internal commitment and supports qualities to espouse	Discuss to discover with spouse and children your mission statement then document. Discuss, reflect and document things you all desire and will commit to doing together. Discuss, reflect and document qualities your family wants to display to everyone all the time		
	75	Marriage / Spouse	A tool to help you and your spouse be the best spouses you can be	Facilitates clarity and understanding of your and your spouse's needs and commitments to each other	Each spouse reflects, documents and shares 10 things important to them. Reflect, share and document things both commit to for your relationship		

#	Page #	ITEM	WHAT IT IS	THE PURPOSE	HOW TO USE	PRIORITY L/M/H	ACTION BY
	77	Kids	A tool to both teach the power of, and do, goal setting with your kids. And tools and processes to become aware and intentional about your family life	Promotes family unity, opens dialogue with and teaches your children to appreciate the power of goals, and supports creation of a highly successful family	For each child, complete with them a list of goals. Discuss and list: things you and your family can and should do together, areas of improvement, and greatest family blessings		
	81	Grandchildren	Tools and processes to have a highly successful extended family – very similar to Kids section	Promotes and teaches your grandchildren to appreciate the power of goals, the wisdom of age and the blessings we have	Help your grandchildren complete a list of goals and activities to enrich your extended family and take stock of those things around you		
	82	Extended Family	A process to discover and document important people, their roles in your family and what needs & priorities you can help them with	Promotes unity and connectivity amongst your extended family by building trust and relationships through meeting them at their needs	Reflect, discover and document extended family members and discuss and document how best you can meet them at their needs. This can be an ongoing exercise as needs change and new relationships are built		
	83	Friends	A tool to list your closest friends and their positive effect(s) on your life	Brings awareness of your closest friends and how you can enrich their lives	Reflect, identify and document your closest friends and their corresponding positive influence – note their priorities and give thought as to how you can enrich their life and help them		
	Goals - important when pursuing personal or business affairs, as they provide and drive: clarity, focus and execution						
	86	Perfect Month	A process to discover what your perfect month looks like	Once you have taken the time to determine and describe your perfect month you have specific goals to work towards	Start by reflecting on your perfect weekday and weekend, working towards a full month - include specifics on work, travel, home, life, exercise etc.		
	89	Balance Wheel of Life (See individual components below)	A process to help you manage balance as you manage life	While you are not likely to achieve perfect balance in your life, the ongoing exercise of managing balance will help you be more effective overall	Reflect on each of the following 6 categories described and listed below		
		Spiritual	A tool to discover and record your spiritual mission statement and goals	Helps guide and give direction	Establish a spiritual mission statement - list your spiritual goals and accompanying key word(s)		
		Social	A tool to discover and record your social mission statement and social goals that lead to a healthy happy and balanced life	You need to be social in order to live a healthy balanced life, allowing you to be effective in other life areas	Establish a social mission statement - list your social goals and accompanying key word(s)		

#	Page #	ITEM	WHAT IT IS	THE PURPOSE	HOW TO USE	PRIORITY L/M/H	ACTION BY
		Education	A tool to discover and record your educational mission statement and educational goals	By continually expanding your mind, growing your vocabulary and improving your thinking you will impact and serve more people	Establish an educational mission statement - list your educational goals and accompanying key word(s)		
		Home & Family	A tool to discover and record your home & family mission statement and home & family goals	Facilitate an atmosphere of communication, openness, trust, faithfulness and commitment where your family can thrive	Establish a home & family mission statement - list your home & family goals and accompanying key word(s) – take time to set goals as a couple and/or parent (page 96 and 97)		
		Physical & Health	A tool to discover and record your physical & health mission statement and physical & health goals	Health is one of life's four Valuables and is critically important to having a satisfying productive life	Establish a physical & health mission statement - list your physical & health goals and accompanying key word(s) – refer back to previous health assessment (page 18)		
		Financial	A tool to discover and record your financial mission statement and physical & health goals	Financial success translates into peace of mind, security, true freedom, pleasure and the ability to serve more people	Establish a financial mission statement – list your financial goals and accompanying key word(s)		
	92	Vision/Results Board (Level 2)	A tool to facilitate the creation of your vision board - a visual representation of goals in your life	A vision board provides inspiration and motivation every time you look at it	Reflect and list, then collect pictures and items that represent things you are striving for – Use Tony's example as a guide (page 82)		
		SECTION 3: MASTERY (LEVEL 3)					
		Who I Am Personally – gain clarity on the various elements that make up who you are and want to be					
	95	Talents	A tool to identify your top talents	You always want to focus on your strengths not your weaknesses. Using this tool allows you to discover your top talents and strengths, so you can focus and spend more time on these	Ask and document what other people in your life see as your top 3 talents and strengths		
	96	Personality Styles	Personality assessment using the DISC method	Identifies your dominant personality and gives you insight into how and why you relate to other people the way you do.	Go to www.personalityinsights.com and take the assessment		
	100	Personal Events of Great Meaning	An ongoing list of happenings that have had great meaning or impact	Encourages, records and enables us to learn from the past to create a better future	Start by listing 5 events and continue using this tool by adding items throughout your lifetime		
	102	Schools and Places of Influence	A tool to identify & list schools, institutions, organizations and churches and the impact they had (and have) on your life	Allows you to identify people, experiences and situations in order to know yourself better and discover "why" you do what you do	List the schools, institutions, organizations and churches and the corresponding impact it had (and has) on you		

#	Page #	ITEM	WHAT IT IS	THE PURPOSE	HOW TO USE	PRIORITY L / M / H	ACTION BY
	103	Personal Daily Standards	A process to discover and list your personal standards that help you run a happy and healthy life	These standards will have a direct impact on how the world perceives you as a person, and will help as guides to run a happy and healthy life	Spend time reflecting and clearly define your personal standards and any other items that are important to you running a happy and healthy life		
		Who I Am Professionally – gain clarity on the past, present and future elements that make up who you are, and want to be, professionally
	104	Business Experiences/ Professional History	A tool that lists a chronological history of your professional life and experiences	Allows you to reflect on your professional career to trigger ideas, best practices and inspiration, in order to bring more value to your world today, and awareness of how these can influence and impact your future	Document chronologically your career history, experiences and professional life		
	106	Ideal Professional Situation	A process to identify the characteristics of, and specific ideal professional situation, clients and/or customers	When you identify characteristics of your ideal client / customer you get a clearer understanding of where to look for this person and how to bring more value to their world	Identify and make a list of your ideal professional situation and client / customer characteristics, make a list of specific companies and individuals and then determine how you can bring them value. Note: This tool is aided by completing previous items in this section		
	107	Business Standards	A tool to identify standards by which you run your professional life	To become aware of and selectively shape your business standards to intentionally impact how the world perceives you	Spend time thinking about and clearly define your business standards – use Tony's personal list (page 37) as a guide to help you		
		Life Guidelines – gain clarity on the way you currently, and want to, operate your life
	109	Thankfulness	A tool to identify and list the things you are thankful for	Remembering the things you are thankful for give life joy, meaning and ultimately purpose, and are powerful tools for defeating discouragement	Thoughtfully remember and list the things you are thankful for		
	110	Favorite Books of Impact	A fingertip list of your favorite books and their main takeaway(s) that impacted your life	To provide a central source of books with the learning, knowledge and guidelines they provided for moving forward as you strive to be your best	List the books and include the key takeaway(s) and / or core concepts of each		
	116	Raving Fans	A list of your best clients, and their contact information, who support you, hire you, refer other people to you and genuinely like you	To give you encouragement and evidence of the impact you have made in other people's lives, and provide a list of people you can contact when you need help	List your best clients who support you, hire you, refer other people to you and genuinely like you, then keep this list close as people you can contact for help (and be ready to reciprocate)		

#	Page #	ITEM	WHAT IT IS	THE PURPOSE	HOW TO USE	PRIORITY L / M / H	ACTION BY
	117	People of Influence (POI)	A tool to create a fingertip list of contact info, their influence in your life, of people with whom you have developed a respected, trusted and thriving relationship	Provides a list of people who may be able to offer assistance to you personally and/or professionally	Reflect, identify and document 12 - 20 people who have an impact on your life and their contact information – note their priorities and give thought as to how you can enrich their life and help them		
	118	Advisors	Processes and tools to identify the people who can help guide you in the right direction and make important decisions	Advisors can uncover blind spots, sometimes motivate you in ways others are not able to, guide you in the right direction, and help you make important decisions	Use the processes and tools in this section to reflect, discover and document the people that you would like to have as coaches, mentors and informal board members		
	121	My Life Team	A tool to discover and document those people in your life who are members of your Life Team - a master list of people helping you make things happen	Brings awareness of how top performers have a top team they can rely on	Identify and make a master list of your Life Team members, their corresponding impact and/or valued characteristics, and determine how you can bring them value. Note: This tool is aided by completing the previous tools and processes in this section as they facilitate identification of your Life Team members		
	122	Intentional Congruence	A process to create a visual understanding of how various influential people and organizations fit into your life personally and professionally	Clarity on gathering the correct people and organizations can help you identify and stay focused on your own High Leverage Activities more consistently	Create a list of people who are influential to you in various ways and then create a mind map that depicts their relationship(s) to you and their sphere of influence – you can use Tony's example as a guide (page 56)		
Goals - important when pursuing personal or business affairs, as they provide and drive: clarity, focus and execution							
	124	10 Times as Valuable	A process to describe focused activities that over the next 2 years would make you 10 times more effective	By becoming more effective you increase your value, and thereby increase your impact and earning power – this will translate into less hours needed to create more value and/or money (i.e. Higher efficiency)	List the people and actions that answer the question: "I will become 10 times what I am now in two years by: being disciplined, determined, confident, persistent & focused on the following points" – this exercise will likely take several sessions and much time, and will greatly be aided by your completion of other sections in this DYOL manual		

#	Page #	ITEM	WHAT IT IS	THE PURPOSE	HOW TO USE	PRIORITY L / M / H	ACTION BY
	126	Likeness Matrix	A tool to record the companies, organizations and people, and their corresponding characteristics, values and distinctions that you want your life to mirror	Thinking about and seeing other companies, organizations or people who have and do what you want brings clarity in order that you can focus on the specifics you want	List the companies, organizations or people and note the specifics you would like to duplicate		
	128	Home Improvement	A list of the home improvements you would like to accomplish in the next 1 to 5 years	Documenting what you would like to add, improve or remodel can draw you towards that accomplishment and will give you both a budget and a sense of each items' priority	List inside and outside improvements and an estimated budget for renovations you'd like made to your home. Include a priority rating now and/or checkmark once completed		
	129	Timeline of My Projected Life	A process to map out the major events that will, or that you want to have, happen over the course of your remaining life	Brings clarity and a sense of reality that we are only alive a relatively short period of time and we want that time to be full of impact	Fill in major events that will, or that you want to have, happen over the course of your remaining life – include your estimated age and year of achievement		
	130	Travel	A tool to list the countries, cities and places you have been and those you want to experience	Seeing the world provides life changing experiences and alters your perspective on life – this list will help "pull" you to these places so you can grow	Reflect and list the countries, cities and places you have been and want to experience in the future. Remember to include your "why" for all future list experiences		
	132	Top 100 Life Goals	A tool to discover and document your ongoing achievement of your personal "bucket list" – this list will evolve over time	There is power in a written list of goals and even more so when we have clarity on "why" we desire a thing. It is also encouraging to be reminded of those goals we have already achieved	Begin listing your top 100 goals in no particular order – these items will evolve as you change over time and you will likely have to come back to this list a few times to complete your initial top 100		
	137	Vision/Results Board	A tool to facilitate the creation of your vision board - a visual representation of goals in your life	A vision board provides inspiration and motivation every time you look at it	Reflect and list, then collect pictures and items that represent things you are striving for – Use Tony's example as a guide (page 82)		

Conclusion - my hope is that this tool has helped and challenged you... to think deeper so you can Design Your Own Life and live an Ultimate Life – Tony Jeary

Glossary: Top Tony Jeary Coined Phrases

- **3-D Outline™:** A powerful outline format that includes the What, Why, and How aspects of a presentation and is used for shortening the meeting planning process (ask about TJI's 3-D Outline™ Builder Software).

- **Audience Champion:** A person in the audience who will openly support the presenter and reinforce his or her message.

- **Breathing Space:** An opportunity to direct the attention of the audience away from the presenter in order to involve the audience more through a change of pace, and to give the presenter a moment to collect his or her thoughts. Examples include showing a video, directing someone else to comment, or having audience members write something down – so their eyes come off the presenter for a few seconds or a few minutes.

- **Clarity, Focus, Execution:** The three core principles for Tony Jeary's Strategic Acceleration methodology.

- **Critical Success Factor Template:** A summary of the key questions and answers required to achieve the highest performance in an important situation. Can be an effective tool for a leader to manage accountability.

- **Daily Performance Standards (DPS):** A concise list of operating procedures intended to provide clear direction relative to expected behavior and energy-spend by an organization's team members.

- **Elegant Solution:** Being so clear on what you want to accomplish that three to five objectives can be simultaneously met through a single action.

- **FPHESS:** Six areas of Designing Your Own Life goal-setting - Financial, Physical, Home Life, Education, Social, and Spiritual.

- **High Leverage Activities (HLAs):** The base methodology of Tony Jeary's bestselling book Strategic Acceleration; HLAs are efficient actions that result in the most valuable outcomes.

- **Life Team:** A group of hand-picked individuals who help you make decisions and execute. Examples could include your spouse, executive assistant, coach, mentors, colleagues, readers, driver, lawyer, trainer, CPA, etc.

- **MOLO (More Of, Less Of):** A simple exercise to help an individual or organization identify what they need to eliminate so they can focus on what matters most. An evaluation of what should be done More Often and Less Often will ensure time is best invested on proactive, productive High Leverage Activities (HLAs) instead of on time-wasting, less effective tasks. Top leaders model self-reflection and continuous improvement.

- **Operational Mastery:** Performing at the top level, better than great, often leading to extended value of an organization of any size.

- **Planned Spontaneity:** Being so prepared you can respond to an audience in impromptu fashion. The better prepared you are the more spontaneity you can bring to your meetings and presentations with confidence.

- **Presentation Arsenal:** A battery of weapons that consists of quotes, stories, statistics, printed and other visual material, wardrobe, electronic files we keep, and anything of substance that can help us make future presentations more colorful and effective.

- **Presentation Universe:** All the presentation opportunities in a person's daily life, both personally and professionally.

- **Production Before Perfection (PBP):** The principle that we must not allow the fear of potential missteps to prevent us from taking effective action now.

- **Strategic Acceleration:** Tony Jeary's proven methodology that helps people get clear, stay focused, and efficiently execute relevant, High-Value activities, thereby delivering results and success faster.

- **Strategic Cascading:** The well-considered, consistent filtering down or across of messages throughout an organization or group (for instance, from a top executive down to his/her direct reports, down to their direct reports, and so on). Messages can also cascade across to other departments, and sometimes even upward in an organization.

- **Strategic Presence:** A leader's "personal brand," lived out through actions and words, that compels others to support objectives.

- **Verbal Surveying:** Asking questions of the audience during a presentation to obtain usable feedback and then adjust accordingly (i.e., speed up or slow down for more or less detail).

About Tony Jeary

Tony Jeary is a results strategist. Many call him The RESULTS Guy™ because of this simple fact—he helps clients get the right results faster. He is a unique and powerful facilitator and subject matter expert who has advised over 1,000 clients and published over forty books. His studio process of live note taking, combined with his *Strategic Acceleration* methodology, is a secret weapon for his special clients. Tony has invested the past 25+ years developing facilitation processes and systems that allow him and his team to accelerate results, doing planning meetings in a single day, and producing results that often take days, weeks, and months in a single eight-hour session. That's a rare gift.

The world's greatest CEOs recognize the importance of thinking, strategy, and communication; and many seek Tony for all three of these. He's a gifted encourager who helps clarify visions.

The primary goal of all leaders is to enhance value and communicate their vision effectively so that their teams can execute that vision in the marketplace. Tony personally coaches presidents and CEOs of Walmart, TGI Friday's, New York Life, Firestone, Samsung, Ford, Texaco, and SAM's; even those on the Forbes richest 400 engage Tony for his advice. Tony personally helps these top leaders: define their goals; accelerate their opportunities; create, establish, and build their personal brands and careers; deliver powerful paradigm-shifting presentations; grow their leadership abilities; and accelerate the right results faster! He and/or his whole firm can be booked through his business manager. Tony Jeary International can be retained to do amazing things to support accelerated RESULTS.

What Can Tony Jeary International Do For You?

CULTURE CHANGE

We change company cultures. *Strategic Acceleration* is a methodology that gets the right results faster for selected clients that have a true appetite for advancing their vision to reality quicker. Our *Strategic Acceleration* methodology is foolproof because it's not theory, academia or new. It's proven, based on real results and works every time. Please Watch the 90 second video on "Change Your Thinking, Change Your Results" at changeyourthinkingchangeyourresults.com. We get results!

STRATEGIC PLANNING

Let us work with you to develop a customized strategic plan for more clarity, focus, and execution, hence more accelerated results! We develop powerful plans in a single day that take most people three days minimum and often weeks. We have a custom-built Strategic Acceleration Studio designed specifically for this offering.

RESULTS COACHING

Having coached many of the world's top CEOs and earners, Tony understands the need for speed in today's marketplace. Benefit from 20 years of best practices from the best of the best. If you operate an organization that has millions to be made, and you're interested in sharpening your executive leadership effectiveness, let's talk.

CULTURE-CHANGING WEB TRAININGS

Most organizations struggle with weekly meetings and poor email standards, resulting in too many meetings and too many emails, costing valuable time. Results are dramatically being hurt because of people operating in overwhelm. Tony has taken his expertise and developed simple 45-minute web trainings that can save thousands of non-productive hours for an organization and greatly impact results. Let us discuss impacting your culture. Subjects include (among others):

Email Effectiveness
Engagement
The Art of Results
Influence

Meeting Mastery
Change Your Thinking
Time Effectiveness

Keynote Speeches

Tony is available for unique keynote experiences that dramatically impact audiences of all sizes. Topics include *Strategic Acceleration* and *Leverage*, among others.

Other Books By Tony

Change Your Thinking, Change Your Results	changethinkingchangeresults.com
Strategic Acceleration	strategicacceleration.com
Business Ground Rules	businessgroundrules.com
Ultimate Health	ultimatehealth-book.com
Life Is a Series of Presentations	mrpresentation.com
How to Gain 100 Extra Minutes a Day	tonyjeary.com
Designing Your Own Life	tonyjeary.com

To discuss how we can bring value to you and your organization, email us at info@tonyjeary.com or call us at 817.430.9422.